THE
TRANSITION
MISSION

A Green Beret's approach to transition from military service

HERB THOMPSON

This book is dedicated to:

CW2 Jonathan "Big Jon" Farmer

U.S. Army Special Forces KIA, Manbij, Syria

16 January 2019

Below is my speech at Big Jon's 5th Special Forces Group memorial ceremony. It was my last act on active duty. These were the best words I could think of to talk about this amazing man who decided to stay in because he was uncertain about his transition and loved being a Green Beret.

We can now add two minor accomplishments to Jon's illustrious and accomplished life. One, in the last six months, he was the only person in group who figured out a way to make me work. And two, he made me cry for the fourth time since I was ten years old the night that I found out he was one of the casualties in Syria. But really this is not about work; this is about love.

Unfortunately, Jon and I attended too many of these memorial ceremonies here, sometimes sitting by each other out there in the pews. Like every Green Beret, we sat there assessing—what others might call critiquing. Afterward, we would talk about if the firing party was on point, if the chaplain said a good prayer, and of course, we talked about the speeches. Were they too long, too boring? Maybe they were okay, or maybe they were really good. Right now, there's a chance Jon is looking down and saying, "Oh Lord, watch out." Probably the same thing Colonel Powers is thinking too. But there's a better chance Jon is saying, "Buckle your seatbelts, we are going for a ride."

Big Jon was on 5321 TCB longer than anywhere else in group. (Taking Care of Business, for those not in the know.) In speaking about Jon, I'm representing a large number of former TCB teammates. Jon was one of the best human beings I ever met in my life—not one of the hundred or so best, but top one or two—just in case I forgot someone in my life from my younger years. Since hearing about Jon being taken away from us, I have spent a good amount of time grieving and reflecting. I was thinking Jon might have been the perfect human being, and then I remembered... Jon sucked at combatives. For a man who could pick up this first pew—with all of the brass sitting on it—if you got him in the fight house, he could not fight his way out of a wet paper bag. So, he was as close to perfect as one could be.

Jon was not just a special Green Beret; he was an amazing husband and father. When we were in Lebanon years ago, we got to take one day a week to do cultural excursions. It was a chance to get a good meal and visit an interesting site. For Jon, what he heard was "shopping excursion." Without fail, Jon would have talked with our Lebanese hosts about a winery to stop at. While we would go see a site, he would buy a few bottles, bring them back to the team house, and not drink them. This went on for a while until I had to ask him what the deal was. He said he knew Tabitha was at home waiting for his return, and he knew it would make her happy if he brought back some wine. He looked forward to playing with the kids and enjoying some quiet time with her. I said, "Okay, Jon. That makes sense." But the bottles started to add up: 20, 30, 40... If you want to know how many bottles fit in a standard size, black tough box, or how many bottles Jon could buy for Tabitha in two months—the answer is about 60.

Jon was a great Green Beret. He excelled. What few know is Jon almost got out of the Army four years ago. We would talk like only those who have been in close combat and who have children and a wife at home can understand. What's the right thing to do? Be home with family or be one of the few that keeps our families safe? We would have these talks regularly. I would ask him, "Where are we at today, Jon?" And he would say, "51–49 getting out." The next time it may be "52–48 staying in." I would ask him the number, and then we would discuss how or why it changed. At one point, his score was 80–20 getting out. One day, much to my surprise, he said he was reenlisting. We talked. He loved being a Green Beret. He loved the men he worked with, and he worried that he couldn't provide the same quality of life for his family if he got out. Most importantly, he wanted Tabitha and the kids to be safe and not have to deal with the evil that we face overseas.

I stand here filled with immense sadness and honor as my last act in the Army is to tell you that Jon made me a better person. I'm far from the only one he affected this way. In true Green Beret fashion, he was a force multiplier. For Manoj, it was mentoring him to pass his first course as a new guy to the team and impressing Wharton with his letter of recommendation. For Pat, it was giving him wise counsel and believing in him. For Matt, it was mentoring him when even Matt didn't realize that was what he was doing. The list goes on for the men and families of Third Battalion. Jon helped many become better Green Berets and people. To us, Jon was a giant presence physically, but his heart was so much larger. Tabitha, Mr. and Mrs. Farmer, the Farmer family—that's the legacy he left behind here at 5th Group.

Big Jon will live on inside all of us, inspiring us to be better Green Berets, spouses, parents, and people. 5th Group, the United States of America, and the world would be a lot better off if we had more Jon Farmers.

I challenge the warriors of this great unit that Jon loved. Let it not end here today. Continue to honor Big Jon and his legacy. Wake up and ask yourself how you are going to make a difference today.

TCB
De Oppresso Liber

Contents

Introduction 1

Transition Truths.. 4

Transition Rules for Success 5

You Are Not Owed Anything! 6

CHAPTER 1: *Where to Begin* 9

CHAPTER 2: *Reality*...................................... 22

CHAPTER 3: *Questions to Begin to Answer* 31

CHAPTER 4: *Setting up LinkedIn*................................. 40

CHAPTER 5: *Leveraging LinkedIn* 50

CHAPTER 6: *What Is Branding?*................................. 56

CHAPTER 7: *The Resume* 61

CHAPTER 8: *Translating Your Skills* 67

CHAPTER 9: *Your Targeted Companies* 81

CHAPTER 10: *It's a Technique*................................. 93

Final Thoughts... 96

Acknowledgments 100

About the Author 102

Introduction

—————

THANK YOU FOR PURCHASING this book and trusting me to offer you my insights on transitioning from military to civilian life.

While this book covers most aspects of the transition, it is not all-encompassing. The knowledge contained in these pages was gained over three years of personal research, experience, and conversations with thousands of people who have come before us and successfully navigated in the private sector.

Why should you pay your hard-earned money and give it a read? Great question and one I would be asking myself. Here is why: Approaching my own transition out of the military after 20+ years, I had no clue as to what I was going to do with the rest of my life. I was lost but knew I had time. What I was sure of was I did not want to become a statistic, and I wanted to be successful. This was not an easy thing to say for a kid who grew up poor and joined the Army at the age of 17. I was not going back to where I came from—not a chance in hell.

I began the process of figuring out civilian life roughly two years out from what I anticipated to be my retirement date. It all began at a marriage retreat sponsored by one of the many great Veteran Service Organizations (VSO) in this country. I spent over three hours on two consecutive nights speaking with Terry, a Vietnam-era Green Beret, who went to Wharton after his service. I began to realize where I was headed. I had never been an adult citizen in corporate America and would have to rely on the skills and knowledge I had gained in the Army. I was an "expert" on unconventional warfare and building rapport. Figuring out how I could use those skills as a private citizen would be my next and, in some ways, most important mission.

In my free time, I pursued my exit from the military and planned like it was a deployment to save the world. And it was. I would save my world. My laptop and I became best friends in studying the problem. I left no stone unturned. I researched careers, the mental aspect of transition, how to dress, life, industries, how people succeeded, why people failed, language, and where in the country I could deploy too. I used my experience of preparing for a deployment to deploy again. I was deploying into America.

During this journey, I spent thousands of hours researching banking jobs on the Internet and LinkedIn. I conducted over 2,000 informational interviews. Yes, I admit that may be overkill—but understand—to me, finance jobs were the tellers at my local bank. I had no clue what the banking industry was. I did not know what I did not know, and I knew I did not know a lot. The only way to figure out how I was going to become successful in my transition was to immerse myself in the process and use the skills I had developed over my time in the military. I knew nothing would be handed to me.

The end result: I was accepted into a graduate degree program at an Ivy League school and landed a job at a top consulting firm. Some may say I overachieved. Others may say I made it to where I belong. What I will tell you is, it was not easy. I had bad days and moments of self-doubt. I was not able to succeed by myself. Countless people have and continue to help me on my journey. It had its ups and downs, just like any other deployment. The constants? Just like on deployments, I kept a positive attitude, worked my ass off, maintained perspective, and built upon small victories.

I have assisted and mentored hundreds of veterans for one simple reason: the more of us who successfully transition and spread around the United States into communities and companies, the better our country will be. Our nation's people need us now more than they may know.

You have been alerted for an assignment. Now is the time to start your transition mission.

Transition Truths

———

► It is your most important mission

► It takes more effort than you realize

► Everyone's transition is unique

► The earlier you start, the better

► Transition is a team sport, but you own the journey

► There are ups and downs

► Thank you for your service, means just that and nothing more

► The more you identify as a service member, the harder it will be

► Transition happens for everyone except for our fallen brothers and sisters

► You are going to make mistakes, learn from them

► You don't know what you don't know

► Success depends solely upon you and your attitude

Transition Rules for Success

► Stay positive

► Smile

► Network, Network, Network

► It's "ME" not "WE"

► Leverage your military experience; you earned it

► Translate your skills and experiences

► Turn assumptions into facts

► Get out of your comfort zone

► Give back

You Are Not Owed Anything!

LET ME REPEAT IT: YOU ARE NOT OWED ANY-THING! It doesn't matter that you're a veteran, or Special Forces, or some other "cool" status. Nothing will be given to you. Just like when you are in uniform, everything will be earned through hard work and dedication. If you have any entitled expectations, then you are failing yourself. That's not the attitude to have. You know damn well that mentality wouldn't work in your unit, and there is no reason to adopt it now.

Let's do a thought experiment. If this hotshot businessman walked into your unit looking for a job, what would happen? But wait, he has this stellar business resume and an excellent education. He seems like a good guy, but he doesn't have a lick of military training. He appears to be physically fit and says he's a good shot. Would he be placed in charge? Made the company commander or a sergeant major? We know the answer to this scenario. Not a chance! His rucksack would be outside before he got started. He would have to earn his place amongst us and start somewhere at the bottom after a vast amount of training.

Unlike this fictional person, a lot of your skills will be useful in the private workforce. You just have to show that to future employers when trying to assimilate into the business world. You have desired skills and experiences; they just need to be translated through the correct prism. I'll tell you more about transferring your skills in a later chapter.

When interviewing, we can expect a handshake and a thank you, but expecting much more than that is insanity. Our veteran brand will give us about 30 seconds of credibility. What we turn that time into depends on us and how well prepared we are to seize the objective. As you transition and approach your next mission, think about what you can give and earn versus what you may think you're owed.

The only thing owed is what you owe yourself. Work your tail off and enable yourself to succeed in your transition. You owe that to yourself!

Let's get started.

1

Where to Begin

E VERYONE, EXCEPT FOR OUR fallen brothers and sisters, will transition out of uniform. You are not alone. Millions of American patriots have had a successful transition before you, so it is within your realm of possibility. Now it is your call to action; it is your time to take control of your journey into the civilian world. I know this change is a little funny for people who have been in gunfights, around explosions, and done numerous other things that an average person would be afraid of. We are scared to leave that behind and join the real world back home.

When notified of an upcoming mission, we begin studying the problem set. The culture, the language, the partner force (mission, capabilities, hierarchy, etc.), the area, the enemy, and the list goes on. Once on the ground, we immediately begin conducting an assessment, building rapport, managing our internal and external expectations, and again, the list goes on. Why wouldn't we use the same approach to transition? We can't expect to know everything about our future careers and get by on instinct alone.

We can use the same approach in our transition. What is the culture of the business world in general, and what is the culture of my targeted industry? Study this on the internet and in networking. We speak a different language than the private sector. Learn the new language and also lose the military jargon. We can even take this down to the micro-level of a specific business. Learn their culture, language, mission, hierarchy, etc. Then we can understand the problem set that we are jumping head-on into.

Fortunately, our military experience gave us a framework to solve problems. In the Army, we call these frameworks a few different things, but the end state is the same. They are Troop Leading Procedures and the Military Decision-Making Process. For this mission, why would we not use the same tools with some twists? We know these processes, we are well rehearsed in them, and they are comfortable for us. Change some terminology, use a little imagination, and boom, we are in business and in our comfort zone.

U.S. ARMY TROOP LEADING PROCEDURES

RECEIVE THE MISSION
ISSUE A WARNING ORDER
MAKE A TENTATIVE PLAN
INITIATE MOVEMENT
CONDUCT RECONNAISSANCE
COMPLETE THE PLAN
ISSUE THE OPERATIONS ORDER
SUPERVISE AND REFINE

Receive the Mission: You will deploy to somewhere in America IOT start a new career and the rest of your life NLT your ETS/retirement date.

Issue a Warning Order: Tell your mission to your family, friends, and unit members.

Make a Tentative Plan: Where do you plan to go, how do you plan to put food on the table, how will you have a sense of purpose? And you can include much more.

Conduct Reconnaissance: Yep, I changed the order up. Start doing digital recon over the internet. Research where you want to live and talk with people who live in that area. If you do this well enough, you can go all-in on your move and not have to conduct site surveys. I did. I made an offer on my new house and went all in without ever having set foot in the area (I wouldn't recommend this ;)). The same process goes for industries and companies.

Initiate Movement: Move to the new location and, hopefully, begin your new job. No—scratch that—hope is not a course of action. You will be going to your new career and home.

Complete the Plan: Initiate all of the items that will be needed for your new home and career.

Issue the Operations Order: Probably not necessary but give it a shot and see how it fits. If you did everything well, it wouldn't look like a military operations order because you will have begun the transformation to becoming a civilian.

Supervise and Refine: Just because you got the new career and are beginning to get comfortable in the new setting doesn't mean you rest on your laurels. Keep refining your plan and ensuring you are on azimuth to your desired end state.

MILITARY DECISION MAKING PROCESS

KEY INPUTS	STEPS	STEPS
• Higher headquarters plan or order or a new mission anticipated by the CDR	**RECEIPT OF MISSION**	• CDR's initial guidance • Initial allocation of time
• CDR's initial guidance • Higher HQ's plan/order • Higher HQ's knowledge and intelligence products • Knowledge products from other organizations • Army design methodology products	**MISSION ANALYSIS**	• Problem statement • Mission statement • Initial CDR's intent • Initial planning guidance • Initial CCIRs and EEFIs • Updated IPB & running estimates • Assumptions • Evaluation criteria for COAs
• Mission Statement • Initial CDR's intent, planning guidance, CCIRs and EEFIs • Updated IPB, running estimates • Assumptions • Evaluation criteria for COAs	**COA DEVELOPMENT**	• COA statements & sketches • Tentative task org • Broad concept of operations • Revised planning guidance • Updated assumption
• Update running estimates • Revised planning guidance • COA statement & sketches • Update assumptions	**COA ANALYSIS**	• Refined COAs • Potential decision points • War game results • Initial assessment measures • Updated assumptions
• Update running estimates • Refined COAs • Evaluation criteria • War game results • Updates assumptions	**COA COMPARISON**	• Evaluated COAs • Recommended COAs • Updated running estimates • Updated assumptions
• Updated running estimates • Evaluated COAs • Recommend COA • Updates assumptions	**COA APPROVAL**	• CDR approved COA with modifications • Refined CDR's intent, CCIRs and EEFIs • Updated assumptions
• CDR approved COA with modifications • Refined CDR's intent, CCIRs and EEFIs • Updated assumptions	**ORDERS PRODUCTION, DISSEMINATION, AND TRANSITION**	• Approved operation plan or order • Subordinates understand the plan or order

Now onto the much more appropriate MDMP for your mission. This process has been used to plan campaigns, wars, battles, and all sorts of purposes in between. Do you mean to tell me it can't be used, with some tweaks, for your transition mission? Hell yeah, it can! It's probably one of the best tools out there to start a framework for your transition. It'll end up looking a lot different by the end, but what better place to start.

Receipt of the Mission: This is the moment you realize transition is happening, hopefully, sooner rather than later. If you're reading this book, then you've met this step. You know you're getting out and are beginning to form what the next mission may be. You now need to figure out your initial guidance on how you are going to eat this elephant called transition and plot out your initial timeline.

Mission Analysis: This is going to be a large part of your process. Guess what? No one is going to give you all the great higher headquarters products (okay, yeah, they were usually lacking) or any great intel products (indeed, they were always lacking). You will have to create these! How, you may wonder? Thank god for the Internet and LinkedIn. Search job, Department of Labor, community, blog, message board, and news websites. You can gather all of the open-source information that you will ever need. Get on LinkedIn. Leverage it to its fullest. More to come on that later. Conduct informational interviews.

What's going to be your problem and mission statements? What are your critical information requirements? Could they be job statistics, necessary credentials, cost of living, etc.? Do you have any information that's essential to you and not to be shared with others? Maybe a hot job lined up? You can make your intelligence prep of the battlefield and keep updating it. We don't know what we don't know. What are some assumptions that we can make that we can turn into facts with more information? I need a PMP certification to get a project management job. I need an advanced degree. I can have a good quality of life at "X" salary. You can fill up pages with these assumptions. What are your criteria for courses of action? Some sample criteria: distance to family, work-life balance, salary, what does the family want, beach or mountains, can you make money doing that, cost of living, intellectually stimulated, responsibility vs. no responsibility, and the list can go on.

COA Development: With all of your information coming into your funnel, develop several COAs. Broaden the plan for each when you get more information, update assumptions, and turn them into facts. COA 1- Banking in Charlotte, COA 2- Management consulting in Seattle, COA 3- Supply chain management in Des Moines. Some sample COAs are VASTLY different. Find what works for you and your family, then develop them out with a broader concept to each.

COA Analysis (War Gaming): From your networking and research, update your running estimates, assumptions, and planning guidance. Put on your red hat and be the enemy. See how Mr. Murphy may rain on your parade. How does your COA compete against roadblocks? Are they real roadblocks or imagined? If you don't get a job for two months after your terminal leave ends, can your plan sustain that? What are your decisive points? Understand at what point will you have to shit or get off the pot.

COA Comparison: You take everything you've done up to this point and grade them. Maybe have an unbiased friend grade them for you. This planning IS NOT done in isolation! How did you rank them, and what is your recommended COA?

COA Approval: Keep refining the COAs and make your decision. Yes, at some point, we cannot put it off anymore. We have to act. Take the lead going out the tailgate of the airplane flying 135 knots at altitude and trust that your parachute opens.

Orders Production, Dissemination, and Transition. So poetic that we end MDMP with the transition. Ensure everyone who needs to know, which is a lot of people. Tell them your plan and what you're doing. Think about family, mentors, connections, old bosses, friends, the mailman, neighbors, companies, etc. It's time to do the transition. We know the plan will change; it's only good until the first shot is fired. But with your planning and preparation, you can more easily adjust and find success now.

Okay, we went through something that should have been familiar: military planning. Now time to get uncomfortable and talk about something unfamiliar. What is your "WHY" or your purpose? If you're like the average service member approaching transition, this is going to be the hardest question to answer and what will drive everything else. You may ask, "What the hell does that even mean?" This is an excellent and reasonable question. We all joined the military for different reasons. Maybe it was out of patriotism, college money, getting away from something, a new beginning, etc. Yes, the pay and benefits were good, but most of us stayed for another reason—to be a part of something bigger than ourselves.

- ► I'm a 23-year-old lieutenant leading a combat patrol in a faraway country, bringing security to an area and taking the fight to evil.

- ► I'm a 26-year-old aviator, dropping bombs on enemy targets, saving American ground forces' lives, or delivering them to the X to conduct a raid.

- ► As a 33-year-old platoon sergeant, I'm setting up a refueling point for the tanks to get their gas and push the assault against tyranny.

▶ I'm a 30-year-old Green Beret training an indigenous force to provide security for their country, and
then I'm leading them outside the wire on patrols.

▶ I'm a 25-year-old recruiter signing people up
to serve their country and follow their dreams
of wearing the uniform of our service.

▶ I'm a 38-year-old warrant officer ensuring that
we meet the standards, get the right parts into
the shop to repair the equipment, and get it
back into operation to help move supplies.

One of these examples may relate to you, but regardless, you were doing something bigger than yourself. It's why you put yourself in harm's way, left your family, put in the blood, sweat, and tears, dealt with the bureaucracy, and proudly wore the uniform of our nation's Armed Forces. It drove you to excel and do unthinkable feats. To deal with suck like those that have not served will never understand. You were a part of the best team this world as ever known.

That is gone now. (More to come on that later.) It's time to find that new "why." This process will not be easy, and you will need to metaphorically hold the mirror up to yourself and look deep inside of who you are. NO ONE will be able to figure this out for you. Others can help inform your decision, but only you will be able to determine what is your purpose in life—the reason you're on this damn planet and how you're going to thrive in life.

I will admit this is not an easy task to even start to wrap your head around. I suggest beginning here. It worked for me and count-less others as well. Ask yourself these questions:

▶ What did you like most in your military career?

▶ Why did you do what you did?

- ► What made/makes you happy?
- ► You had a sense that this was what you were meant to do, even when you were tired and covered in mud. What was it?
- ► What got/gets you out of bed in the morning?
- ► When were the times you drove home at the end of the day with a smile and could not stop smiling?
- ► What moments gave you a feeling of immense pride?
- ► If you died today, what would you be most proud of?
- ► Where can you see yourself getting similar feelings?
- ► What legacy do you want to leave on this planet?
- ► What keeps you up at night because you're so excited about it?
- ► What did you do solely because you had to but not because you wanted to?
- ► How can you equate these answers to $ and a career?

Answering these questions will not happen in one night; it will be a process. The more you figure out these answers, the better you can determine how they fit into a new career. Notice I did not say anything about how much money you want to make, what kind of car or motorcycle you want to drive, how big of a house or houses you want to live in, or how to make someone else happy. The questions are about you and your family, but mainly about you—what is inside your heart and brain. Your motivation to keep breathing oxygen and staying vertical on this planet. What are your dreams?

I want to give you an example. This was for me and only me. You will be different. When I started reflecting on my 20-year career, some common themes kept coming up. I enjoyed helping others. I really enjoyed assisting others in meeting their goals, even if they didn't believe they could. I felt fulfilled knowing I did something for others, and they were going to have a better life because of it. I was happy when I was challenged to the max and given the hardest tasks to accomplish. I liked it when things were ever-changing, and I had to solve ambiguous problems, which is just about everything we do. I loved leading others, but not because I had a piece of cloth on my uniform that said to follow me, but because I had earned their respect and trust to lead us to success collaboratively. It was even better for me when the person didn't realize I was leading them to positive change and results.

Then I looked at what those examples meant in the civilian world. Spotting careers where I would not find those experiences became easy for me. I was able to do this by talking with people in all industries. Once I narrowed down where I did not see my "why," I began to focus on management consulting because I was learning that I could most likely find my purpose in that industry. This realization led me to create my long-term goals and formulate a plan to get there. I'm still on the journey to my end state.

You may have heard about a couple of books that can help you in this process. I in no way endorse these or have any connection to them, but I've read them, and I know many who also have. They were not life-altering for me. Some of my friends had their lives changed after reading these books. One is *Designing Your Life: How to Build a Well-Lived, Joyful Life* by Bill Burnett and Dave Evans, who are engineer professors at Stanford. They break down a process for you to follow that I found a little dry. The process takes reflection, along with doing some tasks over time. Another one is *What Color is Your Parachute* by Richard N. Bolles, which helps you take inventory of your life now and where you want to be. If you find my book useful, you may find their books useful.

The bottom line is that I encourage you to take the time for reflection and ask yourself the hard questions. Talk with others to help inform your decisions and thought processes. If you do not do this, you will either have to be very lucky or, most assuredly, will not have a good transition. Put in the work now to have a better landing later on.

MASTER THE BASICS

We are successful in our missions because we are masters of the basics. Transitioning out of the Army should be no different. So, we have to research, prepare, and master the new basics necessary for us to crush it in the private sector. Below is a task list to master before or while finding your purpose/passion/fire inside/goals.

TALKING ABOUT YOURSELF

This is not an area we are always comfy with. It's okay. The fact that we were Green Berets/Aviators/Grunts/Communications is not a matter of national security. Be a quiet professional, not a silent professional. Share your applicable background. Most of us have experiences talking in uncomfortable situations with tribal elders, militia leaders, and foreign dignitaries. We made it happen and got the mission accomplished. Think of interviews and networking in the same way and be willing to talk about yourself and highlight the appropriate skills.

NETWORKING

We must network to fill our information gaps. We must identify our facts and assumptions. We don't know what we don't know. Networking is the only way to gain this vital information. Build a network and stay engaged with that network. Seek information from all types of people, and just like you did in the military, use your personal filter to see how the information relates to you.

RESUME

We need a resume for our future career opportunities. It doesn't work out well when someone asks for a resume, and we think *oh shit* as we hold our soldier record brief or equivalent. We won't get a job by just submitting resumes to recruiters and hiring managers, but we will need it once we open the right doors for those job opportunities.

DRESS

Tactical cool guy wear is probably not going to cut it in 99.9999% of situations. Study the scenario and dress appropriately. Lose the combat boots. When in doubt, dress one level up. It never hurts to look sharp in a suit with expensive footwear. People in the know will notice if you have classy shoes on or something you probably stole from your father. Corfams are a hell no.

INTERVIEWS

This is an area where we have little to no practice. I never interviewed for a mission or a position of increased responsibility. The Army has a different system in place. But as we transition into schools and jobs, we will conduct interviews. Prepare for these like they are key leader engagements. Know how you are attempting to portray yourself, your goals, and have the proper experiences ready to talk about succinctly.

A CELEBRATION DANCE

Since you are determined, you've prepared, and you know yourself, you will succeed. Have a private celebration dance ready to go. Don't get caught dancing awkwardly by others. Whether that dance is with your family, your dog, a buddy, or yourself—enjoy the moment. Then, thank those that helped you get there and prepare to help others following behind you.

Mastering this list and combining it with your purpose while managing expectations will lead to success.

2

Reality

―――――――――

*How well you transition is how comfortable you are at
being looked upon as a shit bag in your unit.*

—SAID TO ME BY A RETIRED SPECIAL FORCES O-6

THE TRUTH IS YOU should be incredibly proud of your
service to this great country. You earned it through blood,
sweat, tears, and the loss of close friends. No one can ever take your
service away from you. Less than 30% of Americans meet the eligi-
bility requirements to serve in our military. You were one of -30%
who raised their hand and said, "Send me!" You now or will soon
join the ranks of veterans in our country, which is around 17%. Yeah,
the whole one % thing isn't exact, but still, that is a small number of
people who fought for the freedom for our nation.

I say, "Thank you for your service to our nation and way of life."
You will hear a lot of people say, "Thank you for your service." It
means one thing and one thing only: thank you for your service in
the military. You may be thinking other things, but that is always
what it means, nothing more and nothing less. My verbal response
is always "Thank you. It was my privilege to serve and live out my
dreams." I mean that from the bottom of my heart, but internally,
I'm wondering what they are thanking me for. Is it for the unimag-

inable horrors of combat that I witnessed and was a part of? Is it for the enemies that I killed, so they don't have to and sleep peacefully at home at night? Is it for the many holidays and special moments that I missed and will never get back? Is it, "Man, thankfully, you were dodging those bullets and not me"? Is it for the pain I feel every day when I wake up until I go to sleep from a body that was pushed past its limits and broke down because we are not meant to sustain that level of trauma? Is it for the times I'm lost in thought about my friends who are not here anymore because they paid the ultimate sacrifice while their families remain to pick up the pieces?

I never say these thoughts because it does not matter at that moment, but it doesn't mean they don't matter at all. There is a time and place for that. People are genuinely appreciative and being nice. It's our duty to be good troopers and acknowledge their thanks.

What they do not mean is, "Thank you for your service. Because you did such incredible things for our country, I'm going to hand you this amazing job offer and hope to all that is holy that you accept it." It does not work that way! What I'm about to write may be harsh, and if you're offended, well, I'd take a moment to look at what I'm saying unemotionally.

NO ONE REALLY "CARES" THAT YOU:

► Were a Green Beret, SEAL, Ranger, or Raider

► Flew fighter jets or helicopters

► Commanded several tanks, artillery guns, or infantryman

► Made a warship move across the ocean

► Led a battalion, squadron, or flight

► How many times you engaged the enemy or trained to do it

► Which countries you deployed to or prepared to go to

► You got a combat action badge/ribbon

► You received "X" achievement medals and "X" good conduct medals

Like I stated earlier, you should remain very proud of your service and accomplishments. But that does not mean a company will see the value as you do. How do you bring value to the company? In most cases, it is not a direct translation unless it is a highly technical field or in the defense contracting industry. So, no matter how much of hotshot "X" you were in the military or because you were an O-5 or E-8, the new organization is going need to see how you bring value and lower their risk of hiring you.

In most cases, you are not the typical candidate with direct experience that they are used to hiring. They most likely will not understand what your skills and accomplishments are, so it is hard for them to understand how those skills work with their business. That's what I mean by nobody "cares." They will not care enough to hand you a job and say, "Get to work, you hard-charging patriot." They will probably say, "Thank you for your service." And they might ask to hear a story or two (more to follow on that topic), and then see how you can increase their profits and decrease their losses.

Have you ever seen that guy in the home town bar or that character on TV, Al Bundy, who's 55 years old, hasn't had a successful life and is still wearing his letterman jacket or jersey from the time he threw four touchdowns against Valley High to win the district championship? Think there is any way veterans can be looked at the same way by not moving forward? I'm not saying to forget their service. I have a crazy uncle (don't we all, lol), who I have not spoken with by choice for a long time. He was a Marine, and he never fails to tell everyone that "HE IS a Marine," how badass he was, and the great things he did. Well, the truth is, he was kicked out for doing drugs and being a jackass within less than a year in the Corps and never left North Carolina where he was during the 1980s. Despite his failure in the Corps, he never moved past this "service." Amongst some of his other issues, he has been a drunk for my entire life and is unable to hold a job because he is a Marine that knows everything. Perhaps he reminds you of someone who didn't move past their service into the rest of their lives.

The more one self-identifies with their service, the harder their transition out of uniform will be. What I mean is, they get their entire identity from being in uniform. I do not say this in a derogatory manner; it's just factual. You know, like Gunny Highway in the movie *Heart Break Ridge*. Usually, it's the old crusty types that you can't imagine having a normal conversation. They can't walk without marching. They have to check a regulation or schedule to ensure it's an okay time to hit the latrine/head. The military needs these types. They help keep the place on the mission.

You may now be thinking, "Yeah, I know some of these types." Or, "Is this retired service member disrespecting my gung-ho attitude?" If you were thinking the first, okay, you're good to go. If you're feeling the latter, I want to be honest and open that you will have a harder time transitioning. If you wore your uniform home every day and your family doesn't know what you look like out of uniform, it's going to be a significant change. If all your awards, deployments, and badges are on your rear window (no judgment, to each their own), you have some other struggles ahead. You have to acknowledge it before you can address it.

Think of the movie *Shawshank Redemption*. Red says that "Brooks was institutionalized." Heywood disagrees, but Red says, "These walls change a man." The same would go for the "walls" of our bases. If you were inside them for 20+ years, you are going to have an adjustment to make on the outside. This is a fact of life, not good or bad, just reality. Check out that scene. It may make some sense to you.

Some people feel a loss of identity. I will admit I was not one of them. While in the Army, I never got my identity or self-worth from serving. I rarely wore my uniform home. When I deployed, it felt like I was going away on a business trip, and that is how I treated it. I didn't want signs in the airport or yard welcoming Daddy home. That was not my style. I identified as Herb. I only knew and still know how to be me.

I understand that some people get part or all of their identity from their uniforms. Those people need to realize that it is done. It was a part of your life but will not be your whole life. The quicker you come to peace with this in your own mind, the quicker you can transform into a veteran who served. You have much more worth than just the uniform that you wore. Most of us will end up living longer out of service than we were in the military. It's okay. You did your part. Time to let someone else carry the torch. Look inside and realize this period in your life is over. You will always be a veteran. But you are Bill, Sara, Andrew, etc. You are you. You define who you are and what you will become in the next chapter of life. You have not reached your pinnacle yet; more greatness is to come.

The ultimate reality I want to mention, which I believe should be the first sentence of every transition brief is, "Reminder: the gates to the base close the last day you drive out, and there is no turning around." Yep, a little harsh but not far from reality. If you're a retiree like me, you can quickly get back on base and have some benefits/privileges. If you're that young E-6 or O-3, you will have a hard time getting back on base without a military ID card. Then once you're on, you can't use any of the stuff on the post except the streets, parking lots, and grass (if an old crusty E-9 isn't looking ;)). This will be getting slightly better in 2020 as veterans can use the commissary and PX.

Don't believe me? Call up your old unit once you're out and ask for something. See what happens. Go ahead, give it a try. They legally will not be able to help you, as you're no longer on their rolls. Maybe they can give you some Veteran Service Organization's number to call if they know it, but otherwise, the unit will be able to do bupkis, zero, zilch, nada. People need to understand that! Others tell me, "Herb, we have a veteran suicide problem; you can't say that." Yes, we do have a problem, and it is very complicated. But lying to people and saying they will be a service-member for life when they no longer get a paycheck or can use the gosh darn places on base is flat out lying to them. What does that do for someone's mental state when they are in need?

The time to know the truth is now, and then you can find the right places to go for help. There is no shortage of resources to assist veterans as long as we reach out. They don't know we need help unless we speak up. It's okay to ask for help. At the end of 2019, there are over 48,000 Veteran Service Organizations in the United States. Again, we have no scarcity of support as long as we know to look elsewhere (over your old unit). Seek out the VA, the local veteran's groups, or do an internet search.

HUSTLE

As much as I hate sport's clichés, and this will date me a little bit, but when I think of hustle, I think of Pete Rose—nicknamed "Charlie Hustle." You may have seen in him in old clips bowling over the catcher at home plate or diving into second base for a double. He ended his career as the all-time leader in base hits for Major League Baseball. He hustled his a** off. It's no coincidence that he got this record.

Most guys, when they get into Special Forces and walk into the team room for the first time, they are hungry and eager to learn.

They want to be accepted onto the team. Hopefully, they kept that attitude their entire career. That same type of hustle is needed as you transition out of the military.

You need that hustle to build your network and grow your knowledge base. A network does not just show up around you. You have to make it. Being hungry to learn about what you don't know is how you close that information gap. Spend time each day learning about your new mission of transition and learning something new. A great way to do this is by developing your network and appreciating the diversity of thought.

Once you have developed a course of action for your future, hustle to make it a possibility. Whether that is for a specific company or school, work your tail off to give yourself the best shot to land a spot there. The harder you work, the more informed your decisions will be. You will be better positioned to seal the deal and land your coveted position. If it takes 100 phone calls, emails, coffee chats, or meetings—that's okay. It is going to require work and energy from you to keep swinging and not get down because the process is difficult.

When you wake up in the morning, ask yourself, "How am I going to hustle today?" Then kick your tail into gear and get to work. Don't be complacent or accept mediocrity. Before you go to bed, ask yourself, "How did I hustle today?" If you can answer that question every day with a concrete answer, you will be successful.

FIT

How can I tell you if something is a good fit? In 1964, a former U.S. Supreme Court Justice, Potter Stewart, essentially said that he couldn't use words to define pornography, but he knew it when he saw it. The same definition goes for "fit." You will know it when you see or feel it.

I will say this; it's hard to see and feel a fit from a computer or phone calls. You have to go to the business or school to see for yourself. I found it beneficial to talk with numerous people about a place but walking through the doors gives you the ground truth. Don't just take a guided tour, slip away, and talk with folks. Get a feel for the place. See what people walking around have to say. Talk with the janitor, chat with executives, speak with the executive assistants, communicate with everyone you can find.

Ask some tough questions. What would you change around here? Do you enjoy coming here every day? What's the best part about coming to work here every day? How's your day going? Do you like coming to work? Don't be shy about asking these questions. With this information, you can get an honest feel and know if this is the right place.

I would suggest looking for passion. Are the folks in the building passionate about what they do? Positivity is contagious. We all want to be around positive people. Think back to a time in your unit with a person who was Lt. Negative. They drained the lifeblood out of an organization. I'd also recommend turning the ole bullshit meter on and getting an accurate reading. Is it a typical day, or is this when they pulled out all of the camouflage? We have all seen and been a part of dog and pony shows. Follow your instincts.

I'll give you an example of how I determined fit. I was searching for business schools to apply to, and through my research, one school rose to the top of my list. I went for a visit to this fantastic college, and within the first hour, it became the only school on my list. I knew it was a fit! I didn't need anyone to tell me that. I knew it with every bone in my body that this was the place for me. If you paid me $1,000,000 to describe that feel and fit, I would have given you some words, but those words would be inadequate to explain what I felt. I just knew it! The people, the setting, and the energy—it all clicked.

I believe it's important that we all fit. We see how well it works when you put a round peg into a square hole. It's a lot easier to picture round holes and square pegs versus ourselves, but you will feel it and know it in your heart when you are a fit for an organization.

3

Questions to Begin to Answer

N UMEROUS QUESTIONS NEED TO be asked and answered on your transition mission. The list will grow and shrink with more research and networking. Sometimes the answer to one question may generate three new items. It's okay. Knowledge is power and will better inform your decisions.

WHAT DO YOU WANT TO BE WHEN YOU GROW UP?

This is the kind of question I asked myself when I approached retirement from the Army. Honestly, up until that point, I had not thought of anything past my Army goals. Fortunately, through some good luck (hard work and opportunity), I was able to achieve all of my Army goals. But what next?

I started to talk with others who had transitioned, trying to figure out how they decided on their next careers. It was informative, even humorous at times. Listening to these stories, some of which were self-deprecating, gave me ideas. People went into contracting, worked for the government, and an array of other businesses. But the truth was none of them were me, and they couldn't pick my future for me. I had to discover for myself what my next chapter in life would be. A critical point that came up was passion. Those that were happy with their lives were doing something they were passionate about.

So, what the hell was I passionate about, and could I make a living doing it? That became a question I tried to answer almost every day for months to no avail. I read the book I mentioned earlier, *Designing Your Life: How to Build a Well-Lived, Joyful Life*. Another book/tool I used was *Strengths Finder 2.0*. This was useful for identifying my strengths in civilian terms, but still, it didn't tell me, "Hey, be this when you grow up."

After a lot of reflection—I cannot overstate how much thought is important—I discovered what I wanted to do. This didn't happen overnight; it took time. To meet my goals, which I developed over time through research and networking, I decided that I needed an MBA. This gave me a purpose. A goal. Something to strive for. It energized me, and I decided to put all of my efforts into meeting these goals, and my intermediate goal of the MBA from the only school I found a fit with. More on that fit in a later chapter.

The truth that I discovered, probably like many others have before me is, only you can find your purpose. Only you can find your passion. I think it's essential to love what you do, and then it's not work. My military career has felt this way, and I considered it a way of life, not a job. If you can discover that critical piece of information for yourself, you can live a happy life after your transition. You will know it when you find it. I'm not following a "normal" path or one most traveled. But I believe in pursuing my dreams and in taking risks. Once I found my purpose, it was comforting to head out into the unknown.

To answer these questions, look in the mirror. Once you have decided/found/discovered what you want to be, pursue it with everything you have. Leave no stone unturned! Own your journey.

COMMON QUESTIONS

Where am I going to live? Some may stay in their current home near the base. Others will move back to their home area. Others, like myself, are not attached to a particular area and will proceed where we like. For me, it came down to two factors. I moved closer to my family and to where the jobs were.

How am I going to put food on the table for my family and me? If we are not eating, no one is going to be happy. Just like an army runs on its stomach, so does a family. I knew I could get a job to put food on my table. I also had the extra cushion of retirement pay and VA disability compensation to count on.

How much money will I need to make? This is about quality of life. Can I pay my bills, and then how much more will I need to make to live comfortably? Again, I had the cushion and was not concerned with the number I determined I would need. Something to think about here is we get a lot more benefits than we realize in the military. Our health care costs are nothing for us and usually nothing or extremely low for our family. That is not the case if you will need insurance through your new employer; it can get really expensive quickly. Also, you need to think about what you are losing once you are a civilian—your life insurance, all the time off we get, discounts, TSA pre-check for those that will fly a lot, and possibly losing access to the commissary and class-VI, to name a few.

What's going to be my new career? The million-dollar question. (Man, that would be great for a salary.) Finding your why, networking, and translating your skills should inform what route to take on a new career path. Figuring this out along with location and salary will be a primary driver in where your transition mission ends up. A lot of veterans automatically think of project management or operations. Do your research to see what those jobs entail.

What will my work-life balance be? After 20 years of being gone and missing so much of my kid's lives, I decided this was my number one criterion for my next career. It's okay to do that if you can afford to. Not all jobs will keep late hours and have you travel away from home regularly. For work-life balance, you have to decide what you need and want compared to your military career. It may be an adjustment for your family to have you home all the time; hell, it may be an adjustment for you too.

What is my timeline? The separation date is set in stone. You're not moving that bad Mama Jama, so backward plan off of it. The earlier you get to work on your plan, the more prepared your environment will be for a smooth landing. It's a marathon, not a sprint. That being said, it will sure go by FAST!

"How do I translate what I do in the military to civilian terms?" (Special thank you to Lloyd Purswell.) For some, this may be a little easier to do if you had a technical skillset. For a special operator, grunt, cannon cocker, tanker, etc.—this will take some effort to see what skills can translate. Knowing I wanted to do management consulting, I focused on my experiences as a trainer, building relationships, improving efficiencies in organizations, and my ability to operate with all levels, from farmer to 4-star general. Talk with people in your targeted industry and read job postings. You will learn what you need to translate. I guarantee, it won't be how many sorties you flew, combat missions you led, or targets you hit.

LESS COMMON QUESTIONS

What does my family want? If you are a single person without dependents, this will not apply. For those with dependents, do not overlook what the family wants. Don't assume, ask them, and have the discussions. It might not be what you expect to hear. We probably owe it to them to value their inputs after they followed us for our military careers.

What certifications can help me in a new career? Certifications are an easy way to augment your experience. Would a PMP or project management certification through the Institute of Project Management help? Should I get an Agile/SCRM master certification? Is there a license that the civilian job requires like a CFA? Do the research. There are many certifications that every company understands and values.

What's the culture I'm looking for in a company? DO NOT just call them up and ask them. This is like walking up to a stranger and asking, "Hey, what's under your skirt?" or "How well is your marriage going?" Yep, that would be a little awkward. Take a more strategic approach and seek out the information from websites and informational interviews with current and past employees. Sometimes to get an answer to one question, we need to ask other questions. Maybe ask: How is the work-life balance? What is the day to day operations? How is the company involved in the community? Is there growth potential? Tell me about the team you work on? Do you speak with company leadership often? What does diversity look like here? What's the innovation process? How are the benefits? Do they offer flexible work hours? Can I bring my dog to work? These are just a few ideas to get you started in your thinking.

How can I leverage LinkedIn? If you are not leveraging LinkedIn, you are missing out on the best resource available (after this book) for your transition mission. Chapter Four covers this topic.

Which elements of this new chapter in life are most important to my family and me? Am I ranking these elements in a certain way to try to posture to others, so that my transition looks seamless, or I'm making choices that are best for me? (Special thank you to Reece Lodder.) This is your journey, no one else's. No need to be cool or worry about what others think. You need to ensure you are staying true to yourself. #youbeyou

Am I ready to commit to an organization for more than 2 to 3 years, which is what the military has programmed us to do? What do 5, 10, and 15 years look like at this organization? (Special thank you to George Davis.) Are you joining this organization as a stepping stone, or do you want to be there for many years to come? Look for jobs with growth potential, so that you can see yourself working there in 15 years. On the flip side, if you know that it's only going to be two years, that is fine too—as long as you understand that.

UNCOMMON QUESTIONS

How will I get a sense of belonging? Like I said in the previous chapter, we were a member of the best team in the world, and that gave us a sense of brother and sisterhood—like a massive semi-dysfunctional family that we would die for. Are you going to be able to find the same thing? Maybe not solely at your new career, but can you find parts of it?

Find a good team with good people with no egos who are committed to working towards a common goal. It's possible, and you need to look for it.

What will be my new "team"? Who will be that new team? Your new group might be partly fulfilled at work, maybe at a local veterans' organization, or a community club. You don't have to go from being on an excellent team to not having a group at all. We tend to have fond memories of our military service, but we often overlook that we had bad days, and there were people we didn't get along with. Just keep some perspective.

How can I go home at night, fulfilled? Most of the time, when we went home in the military, we knew without a doubt that we had accomplished something, and it was for a greater good. We had this need fulfilled. We were serving our nation. Good people at home and abroad were safe because of our efforts. You may not find the same fulfillment in your new job. Can you be partly fulfilled at work, knowing you're doing something right on a lesser scale? An excellent place to find some fulfillment for that fire in the belly is helping out with a local service club or giving back to other veterans.

Where will the adrenaline rush come from? You may not think about it, but man, you sure did some crazy things. You were jumping out of planes, driving a convoy through hostile areas, or shooting cool weapon systems. Are you prepared to not do that anymore? There are many unhealthy ways that people turn to for adrenaline. Be aware. You may feel an adrenaline need. Find those healthy outlets to get the blood pressure going.

How will I talk about my military experience? At some point, you will get asked some awkward questions! Did you kill anybody? What was combat like? To a lady veteran, "How did you work with all those guys?" You can imagine the questions. After some standard go-to answers, you can move on about your day. But also give some in-depth thought about what you will say to those who may become closer to you. We need to tell our stories, and the American people need to learn from what we have been through. That does not mean it's a good idea to pull out war story number 2 in the break room or war story number 5 at the company picnic. Be wise and think about what others will hear when you tell a story; the meaning is most likely different than what you intend to convey.

How will I thrive in an environment that may not value me for my service? (Special thank you to George Davis.) Some companies are just not going to value your service or experiences. Will you be okay working in a place like that? What if they appreciate it but not to the extent you feel they should because you're outperforming younger coworkers? Figure out your mechanisms to test this and then figure out a way to get them to see the value of your service. You are your salesperson. We will talk about branding in a later chapter.

Why am I transitioning? (Special thank you to Patrick Perry.) This seems so simple, but so many people are not honest with this one. Only you know the real answer, and whatever it is, it's okay. For me, I had done my 20 years and went through a medical board. That made this question very easy for me. I could no longer physically do what I needed to do as a soldier. This reason for transition made my mental shift a whole lot easier to accept. Even if I wanted to stay, reality said I couldn't do what was needed anymore. I found peace with my decision after years of dealing with an injury.

Am I ready to be a "veteran" instead of a "servicemember"? (Special thank you to Patrick Perry.) A pretty straightforward question, and don't discount it. While finishing this book, I'm watching a news program about how U.S. Forces killed the leader of ISIS, and I know some of my guys are over there. Yes, I had about a one-second thought of, "Damn, I wish I were there." That quickly shifted to, "Man, I'm glad we have guys like that, and I'll be proud to one day tell my kids I served with such men. I had my fun in the sun. Now it's someone else's time to carry the load.

This is not the be-all and end-all list of questions to ask yourself. They are meant to get your juices flowing, and the brain working on a variety of concerns regarding the transition. I guarantee these will generate further questions. Keep reflecting and networking to answer them. It's okay if you don't know the answers right now, but at some point, you have to know.

Critical reminder: this is not a perfect world. Not everyone lands the dream job right out of transition. That is not how life works. Sometimes we need to take a position to take care of ourselves and our family. Maslow's hierarchy of needs will rule the day: physiological, safety, love and belonging, esteem, and self-actualization—in that order. Once we have the food, air, water, and shelter for the physical needs, then we can move on to being safe and focus more of the touchy-feely needs. Don't get confused that living a dream is more important than your kids having clothes on their back and food in their little tummies. It's okay to put the goals on pause to take care of what needs to be done now. If you can make that a building block towards your dream, then that is even better. I love my company and where I work, but it is not my dream job or my end goal. It is a step towards getting to my dream job, which in my planning, I decided I had to take to get where I want to be.

4

Setting up LinkedIn

———

ASIDE FROM THIS BOOK, LinkedIn is the #1 asset to use in transition. LinkedIn gives you the ability to meet and connect with people you would have zero chance of knowing otherwise and is critical for networking and discovering information. Picture it, you are at Ft. Bragg or Camp Pendleton, but you plan to move to Seattle or Chicago. How often do you think you are making trips up there to attend networking events and job fairs? The time and costs will add up quickly. However, with LinkedIn, you can do that every day whether you are on base, home, or forward deployed with an internet connection.

You can't just sign up, and people flock to you. I think you get that point by now. You need to use it properly to leverage it for maximum gains. I'm a believer. I was not living in Washington, DC, but planned to move to this area. I used LinkedIn extensively to network in my new city and into my targeted companies.

Note: sign up for the year free premium membership on LinkedIn. I would recommend doing this 6–9 months out from transition. If you're rolling with extra cash, do it when you feel it is best. The premium package gets you InMail options, more profiles when you search, additional filters to search with, expanded profiles, and more.

YOUR PICTURE

It should be a smiling professional-looking picture in professional business attire that shows only your head and shoulders (headshot). Let people see what you can be. Do not be in uniform or tactical gear. That is already what a hiring manager sees you as.

BACKGROUND IMAGE

This is free marketing space, don't let it go to waste. Show something about yourself or where you want to be. It should be professionally related to what you want to do, but don't be afraid to show a little personality unless it would be off-putting. In the background below, she is showing people that she was moving to NYC upon transition.

LOCATION

If you're remaining in the same location that you are in when you leave the military, this is a simple solution—put that city. However, if you're moving to another city (like I did to DC), then put the new city. It will work better in networking if people see you in the new location. You may not come up in their searches, or they may wonder why someone from Tampa is trying to connect with them in Seattle. We are trying to show the new us, not what we used to be.

HEADLINE

The headline is what everyone sees along with your name. Leverage this to tell people who you are and where you are going. DO NOT put transitioning soldier or your military titles. People are not interested in seeing that. It's the old you. Put the type of jobs you're looking for, maybe when you're available, or what drives you. Tip: If you use an iPhone, you get an extra 100 characters.

Eric Horton Transition Hacker · 1st in
2019 Tennessee Top Veteran Leader | Corporate & Individual Branding | Veteran Initiatives | Driven by Passion
Greater Nashville Area, TN · 500+ connections · Contact info

Steve Hauck · 1st in
I help PNW manufacturers achieve operations and supply chain excellence.
Olympia, Washington · 500+ connections · Contact info

ABOUT

This is like a summary, or your elevator pitch. I would recommend keeping it short to a paragraph or two. No need for an essay. Most people are not going to take the time to read a lengthy summary. Think about what you're attempting to brand yourself as (more on branding later). Look at what others in your targeted industry have put in this section. Let that inform what you put in yours.

EXPERIENCE

Put your experiences in civilian terms that are easily understandable. Do not just copy evaluations or award bullets; you may be able to use these with some updates. Most evaluation and award bullets are not well-written and don't tell the full story that you want to portray. Be mindful if you are putting your previous rank anywhere, officer vs. enlisted or junior vs. senior officer. Some biases exist. Oh, you're a Junior Military Officer (JMO). Oh, you're enlisted, you will be a worker bee/laborer. Oh, you're a Colonel and too senior for our positions.

Like I stated earlier, the cool guy stuff in combat and jumping out of planes is not going to work. I left mine pretty bland due to not being directly translatable and classification issues. My resume is much more robust.

Operations and Strategy Leader
Sep 2013 – Mar 2015 · 1 yr 7 mos

Directed operations and strategy for a client focused team around the Middle East.

Operations Leader
Dec 2009 – Sep 2013 · 3 yrs 10 mos

Worked with many clients in numerous countries to improve their performance.

EDUCATION

List all schools you got a degree from, no need to include GPA. Add any relevant organizations from college. You never know when they will help out. Also, list any graduate or transition programs you attended. This helps spread your network.

Education

 Cornell University
Master of Business Administration - MBA
2019 – 2021

 The Tuck School of Business at Dartmouth
Next Step: Transition to Business
2018 – 2018

An executive education certificate program designed for military veterans and elite athletes. Taught by Tuck's leading faculty, the program focuses on developing and honing business skills in strategy, marketing & communications, financial analysis, leadership, and more.

 Southern New Hampshire University
Bachelor of Science - BS, Business Studies in Business Administration
Activities and Societies: The National Society of Leadership and Success

LICENSES AND CERTIFICATIONS

List any certifications that you may have. PMP, SHRM, SCRM, Security+, etc. You can add your clearance if you are comfortable with that being out in the public eye.

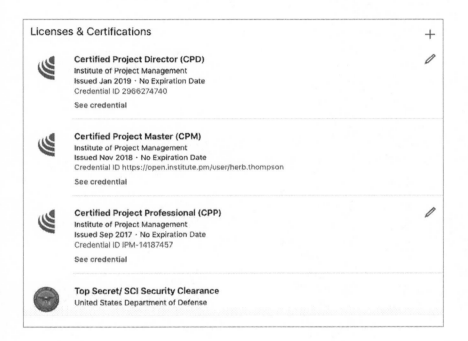

SKILLS

Input no more than 25 relevant skills. It's not beneficial to have all 50. Are these relevant to what you want to do in the future? Security, military, DOD, etc. List skills that people already have in your desired career field. Yes, it will take a while to get others to endorse your skills, but it will be worth it in the long run. People do searches for these. If you know someone, endorse the skills that you know they have. It's good karma and likely to come back around.

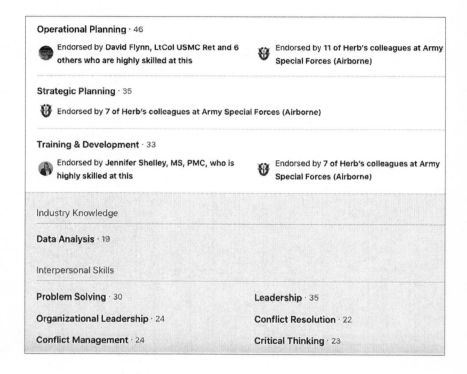

ENDORSEMENTS

These endorsements show others that people value you and think highly of you. They are very nice to have. Give recommendations to people you know and have worked with or to someone who mentored you. There is a good chance they will return the favor.

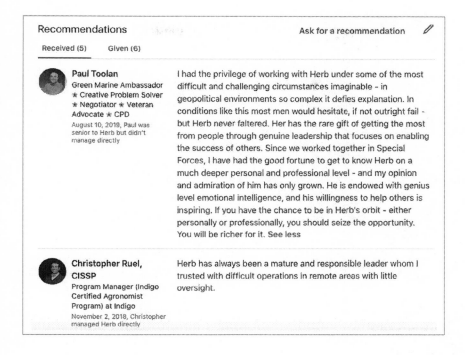

Recommendations   Ask for a recommendation

Received (5)   Given (6)

Paul Toolan
Green Marine Ambassador
✻ Creative Problem Solver
✻ Negotiator ✻ Veteran
Advocate ✻ CPD
August 10, 2019, Paul was
senior to Herb but didn't
manage directly

I had the privilege of working with Herb under some of the most difficult and challenging circumstances imaginable - in geopolitical environments so complex it defies explanation. In conditions like this most men would hesitate, if not outright fail - but Herb never faltered. Her has the rare gift of getting the most from people through genuine leadership that focuses on enabling the success of others. Since we worked together in Special Forces, I have had the good fortune to get to know Herb on a much deeper personal and professional level - and my opinion and admiration of him has only grown. He is endowed with genius level emotional intelligence, and his willingness to help others is inspiring. If you have the chance to be in Herb's orbit - either personally or professionally, you should seize the opportunity. You will be richer for it. See less

Christopher Ruel, CISSP
Program Manager (Indigo
Certified Agronomist
Program) at Indigo
November 2, 2018, Christopher
managed Herb directly

Herb has always been a mature and responsible leader whom I trusted with difficult operations in remote areas with little oversight.

ACCOMPLISHMENTS

Put any accomplishments that you have. I would recommend not putting your military awards. The awards by themselves give no context for the reason they were given, the why, or the meat behind them. This is a great place to list additional languages that you speak and organizations that you belong too.

Accomplishments   +

2 Languages   ⌄
   Arabic • French

1 Organization   ⌄
   Special Forces Association

INTERESTS

Leverage this section to follow relevant people and companies in your desired business or industry. Recruiters and hiring managers sometimes look at these. It can reveal a little more about you and your thinking. Why not use it to make people think you care about hot topics in business and are smart about the current business climate?

URL

Personalize your URL. Don't just leave it as the generic URL with numbers that LinkedIn assigns. Again, we are trying to look more professional and cover all of our bases.

Good: www.linkedin.com/in/james-jones-operations-leader
Not Good: www.linkedin.com/in/james-jones-2348657

SETTINGS

Allow people to see your profile and information. It does no good to hide on LinkedIn. This is the time to shine a spotlight on you.

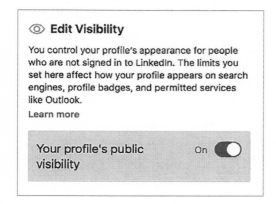

OPEN FOR JOBS

Let recruiters know you are open and on the job hunt. Again, this is not a time to be a shrinking violet.

> **Show recruiters you're open** to job opportunities—you control who sees this.
> Get started

5

Leveraging LinkedIn

Y OU GET OUT OF LinkedIn what you put into it. The more you engage by writing posts, comments, and giving likes, the more your network will begin to spread without you having to search people out. At first, there will be a period where you will need to search people out. An excellent way to do that is to search for everyone you know. Once you have exhausted all of those people, move on to sending connection requests to strangers with similar interests or have someone make an introduction for you. A good method to use is to request a connection from those that comment on your posts.

GENERAL TIPS

- ► Stay positive
- ► Pause, proofread and think before hitting send
- ► **Engage, Engage, Engage**
- ► Build a relationship/connection before an "ASK"
- ► Post about your transition experiences
- ► You get out of it what you put into it
- ► You are your brand

DIGITAL TARGETING/FOCUSED NETWORKING

You may be familiar with targeting in the military. Yes, there is such a thing as non-kinetic targeting. Also, you may have heard about mapping the human terrain. With a small adjustment, you can appropriately use skills that you already built in the military on LinkedIn. You can use the same approaches to conduct focused networking. Ever heard of aim small, miss small? That's right; I know you have. We've all been on a weapons range. If we closed our eyes and shot somewhere downrange, our chances of hitting our target were almost non-existent. However, when we used marksmanship fundamentals and aimed really well at the target, our chances of hits increased greatly. I used the same targeting techniques that I did overseas on deployments with my job hunt. I targeted three companies and landed interviews at each company. The process works!

Think of it as three buckets or areas to target:

Location or locations you are planning to live.

Industry or industries are you planning to work in.

Company or companies that you intend to apply to or learn more about.

Start by using LinkedIn searches to find veterans to send connection requests to. Especially look for ones from your service and career field. Once you have exhausted those efforts or are ready to move on, begin reaching out to non-veterans in your network.

I used a variation of the below template and received a 99.9% response rate. I do not remember anyone not responding, but I'm sure it must have happened, so I'll leave it at that percentage. You can choose to go with a different method or my template. I guarantee this one works. I would often add a line about how they were successful, and it would be great to hear how they were able to navigate up the company ranks.

Their Name,

I'm a (transitioning or retiring) Green Beret (Use the title of your liking. Marine, Naval aviator, Army infantryman, etc.) looking to learn more about your (company, industry, etc.). It would be great to connect and gain any knowledge or insights that you would be willing to offer to help me on my transition.

Thank you for your time and consideration.

Your Name

What I did not do was have an "ask" for more than that. A lot of people will automatically ask for a phone call, a LinkedIn profile review, a resume review, or a job offer. Let's think about that for a minute. First, a lot of people charge for these services. Secondly, you don't know them, and you already want them to take their valuable time to do something for you. (They only have 24 hours in a day too.) Lastly, what would you do if a stranger showed up on your doorstep, knocked on the door, and when you opened the door, they handed you a resume? Then they said, "Hi, I'm (insert name). I'm a transitioning soldier. Will you spend the next 30 minutes looking over my resume. I'll wait right here." At a minimum, that is awkward. You can imagine it going way worse from there. They will think they have a nut-job at the door, and the police are called. Now imagine that person is in camouflage and with their best war face on. (A special thank you to my friend Bill Kiefer for this analogy.) There is no difference from that silly analogy to what people do on LinkedIn without first building a relationship. Yes, the worst case is the person doesn't respond to your connection request or message...... But wait, is that the worst-case? No, it is not the worst case. If this was a company or industry you were targeting, there is a chance they may have a say in hiring you or that someone may ask the hiring manager if they know you—being a veteran and all. Maybe they put your name on an internal, "This person is an idiot/do not hire list."

Take the time and demonstrate patience in building some form of a relationship. Exchange some messages or have a phone call. Then that could be an excellent time to come with an ask. The more significant the ask, the better the relationship should be.

If you follow this process months in advance from wanting or needing a job at a company, it lays the conditions for them to more than likely reach out to you about positions when they become open. Yes, a lot of times, people in the company know about openings before they are posted for the world to see. When you get to that time that you are out of uniform, and you have built some form of a relationship, then you can ask about their job openings, and it can go smoothly.

POSTING CONTENT

This is a hurdle most of us begrudgingly overcome. It may not be comfortable for you. Time to get comfortable with the uncomfortable. You've deployed, engaged, and destroyed the enemy or trained to do it. Now you're scared about a little bit of social media posting? Be comfortable in your own skin, be confident that you are someone with knowledge that can help someone or get your questions answered. The more you post content, the more relevant it will become, and the better you will get at it. Hmm, yep, practice improves your skills. At least try to do it a couple of times a week with some thought put into it. You do not have to become a social media influencer. But just maybe that question you have, one of your fellow transitioning service members has it too or will be put in that situation a week from now. We all help each other and grow together.

Some words of caution: we can't make everyone happy, but something that can appear negative or distasteful will push people away. Think of your brand; branding is covered in the next chapter. If you think your post may be provocative, my suggestion is to frame the issue. Take a moment and think about how someone else may read it. Run your ideas by trusted sources.

POSTING TIPS

- ► Don't be a Silent Professional
- ► Be AUTHENTIC #youbeyou
- ► Be VULNERABLE: show your failures and lessons learned (this will get the most attention and reactions)
- ► Think before hitting send (proofread)
- ► Use popular hashtags
- ► Post regularly

A GREEN BERET PUTTING HIMSELF OUT THERE

(1,000 Cups of Coffee)

6

What Is Branding?

DURING OUR TIME IN uniform, we may not have consciously worried about our brand. A lot of the time, it was done for us depending upon the type of unit we were in or what adorned our uniform. See a SEAL trident, aviator wings, EOD badge, Green Beret, or airborne wings. They had a brand backing them up that people knew they were a part of. I bet most of you worried about your unit's brand. No way was a sister unit going to talk shit to your unit. At a minimum, that led to words exchanged or other shenanigans. You were protecting your unit's brand. When you went out and did excellent work because you didn't want to let your team, squad, or platoon down, you were worried about the unit's brand. I think you get the point.

Did you want other people to know/think you were a shit bag, or did you want to be known as a good soldier, sailor, airman, or marine? Yeah, that's what I thought; you cared about your brand. It was your reputation! That reputation starts at different points in different units. For SEALs, it's in BUDS; for Green Berets, it's in SFAS; for Aviators, it's in flight school; for academy graduates, it's during the first summer at school; for some, it may be Initial Military Training; or for others, it may be at their first unit.

Then you built your reputation through your fitness, mission accomplishment, how you carried yourself, and a variety of other ways.

When you were reporting to a new unit, you don't think the leadership called back to your last unit and asked about you? Remember, they probably asked around your gaining unit to see if anyone knew you. They were asking about your reputation, which preceded you and often stayed behind long after you left. That is your brand, nothing fancy about it. Now how does that look as we transition? Your military experience will be a part of your brand, no doubt about it. Everything you post on social media and every word spoken in conversation with others becomes your brand. But how else can you start transforming that brand?

TRANSFORMING YOUR BRAND

- ► LinkedIn
- ► Social media
- ► Informational interviews
- ► Resume
- ► Job fairs
- ► Networking events
- ► Who you associate with
- ► How you speak
- ► The companies and people you follow
- ► Authenticity
- ► You are your own marketing manager/publicist

INFORMATIONAL INTERVIEWS

What in the world is an informational interview? Much like branding, it sounds like such a complicated term, and it's not. Let's break it down and continue to keep things simple. Drum roll... It's two people (typically two but can be more) having a conversation. OMG, so complicated, right? That is all it is. When you reach out to someone to gain information about something (location, industry, or company), to learn more about the topic and to help inform your decisions going forward, you have an informational interview. It can be on the phone, a virtual chat, in person over a coffee, a cold beverage, or a meal. It could be on a boat ride, a hike, doing an event together, and the list continues. Utilize these chats to turn more of your assumptions into facts. Come with set ideas about the knowledge you are trying to gain. Use your emotional intelligence to figure out when is the best time in the conversation to ask some questions (not immediately after saying hello). Get to know the person a little bit. Have a conversation. Don't just go in asking a bunch of questions.

How was/is your day? How's the family? Work going well? What new project are you working on? Do some research on the person. Remember digital targeting. Find some information that you can leverage, maybe their favorite sports team or pet (ask me about my dog, and I know you did some homework). Perhaps you've been to where they grew up, attended their school, maybe they are a veteran, or maybe you've been to the location you're meeting them at in person. Once the conversation is flowing, you can work in your essential questions. The goal should be for the other person to talk more than you. I'll let you in on a secret, the vast majority of people like talking about themselves; that's not always the case with most transitioning service members. Leverage that to make them feel good and be interested in what they are saying. You might learn something too. When you think the moment is right, throw in a question of your own that you want to be answered. Make them opened ended. That's the key to keeping the conversation flowing. Yes/no questions are dead ends. They lead nowhere. Remember the 5 W's (who, what, where, when, why, how). I know that's six. Don't come with a list of 54 questions and expect all of them to be answered. That sounds more like an interrogation or the worst telemarketer ever. Get what you can, and lastly, see if it leads to another connection. If you played it right, it should usually lead to being connected with one or two more people. That is how you grow your network and get all the information you need!

QUIET PROFESSIONAL VS. SILENT PROFESSIONAL

(How I Viewed Leveraging My Green Beret)

Our culture in Special Forces and unofficial motto is the "Quiet Professionals." We do our jobs/missions not looking for accolades but because we know we are making a difference. But there is a difference between being a Quiet Professional and a Silent Professional. We fail ourselves and our brotherhood when we think we have to be silent professionals. We have stories and experiences to share that are impactful and resonate with people. We cannot be afraid to tell them, to share that knowledge, and inform America.

God bless our brother Seals, but they are neither quiet nor silent. In many cases, this is a reason why they are able to break through barriers when they separate from the military. I'm not saying every Green Beret needs to write a book or start writing their movie script, but we can learn a little bit from our brothers in arms. Being a "SEAL" gives them probably more than 30 seconds of credibility in an introduction. They can then turn that into so much more and lead to opportunities. If we can gain more than that 30 seconds of credibility from saying we're a Green Beret, then that is an opportunity we should take advantage of to open up opportunities after our service.

We are comfortable in the uncomfortable. Masters of Chaos. We need to get over that awkward moment of telling others we are/were a Green Beret. The doors and potential that can be opened are numerous if we allow ourselves to speak freely about who we are. Try it and see the results that happen. You will be amazed at how that can springboard a conversation. Frankly, it's okay to say, "Hi, I'm (insert name), a former Green Beret, and it's nice to meet you." You are not divulging national security secrets by saying you are a Green Beret. You're just identifying a chapter of your life that you have proudly earned.

It's all about branding. You have a brand, and the Green Beret has a brand. These two brands are intertwined. The more we play the silent professional, the more our personal and the Green Beret brand is held back. Elevating your own brand can be a game-changer in transition.

7

The Resume

THE RESUME IS NOT the most critical item, but essential to get your foot in the door. Opinions on resumes are like rectums, and everyone has one. Specific industries have different standards or norms. It is not a CV; leave that for the academic world. Also, if you are pursuing a federal service job, their resume format is very specific, longer, and not covered in this section. I will give a few guarantees with resumes. You may think your first one is great or okay. I will guarantee it sucks. Mine did. Everyone I've ever spoken with had a crappy resume at first. You will not have done a good enough job translating your skills and revealing the relevant information to be hired.

Okay, now that we got that shock out of the way, I'll give you the most significant guarantee of all. No one knows you as well as you know you and what you have done. I hear a lot of people just gathering up some evaluations, awards, and maybe a DD-214 and sending them off to a professional resume writer. I have nothing against these folks who make a living this way. I'm friends with some of them. What they do not know is your passions, the information missing off of those pieces of paper, and who you really are. How can they possibly write your resume well? Yes, they know how to format and what good bullets look like, but they do not know you as you know you.

It is much easier for you to learn the formatting and how to make a good bullet than it is for them to learn all about you.

How can you learn? Research on the internet to start, then leverage informational interviews. Since you were so good at chatting them up, they may review your resume for you. Reminder: just like with everything, it is only one person's opinion. I'll give a story on that in a little bit. Put it into your filter and adjust the resume as you see fit, then continue.

Now I'll give you a big secret that will help you use focused networking to help with your resume. You can't tell anyone. Look around. No one's over your shoulder, right? I used focused networking to establish relationships with people who write/review resumes for a living, some for between $500–$1000 a pop. I was able to get four separate resume writers to review my resume at different times for FREE! All by connecting and building relationships over time on LinkedIn. You will end up with many versions and making tweaks to it along the way until it is the best product.

I want to share a short story about one person's opinion about my resume. One of the first Veteran Service Organizations that I was fortunate to learn about, and that helped me out was the Tuck: NextStep program. (They even paid for my tuition). One of the senior ladies in the organization was my contact, and she reviewed my resume as was standard with their process. She was adamant that I did not put that I was a drill sergeant on my resume. So, I listened to her. It was for all the wrong reasons/biases that one might think would come up. You will look like an asshole (my words), mean, someone who yells and seem downright scary to civilians. I stated my argument for keeping it, and we disagreed. This is where you own your journey. I understood her point, which is very valid. Yes, they are valid for the drill sergeants who are reading this. However, I was not selling the drill sergeant experience that way. I was showcasing the ability to train and transform America's sons and daughters into soldiers. Plus, I was the Army Drill Sergeant of the Year, gaining important experience working under a 4-star general. Remember, I was targeting management consulting. Because it was not important to me, I used to not tell people I won this award and performed the follow-on duties, even though I was the only person in the history of the Army to have won Army Drill Sergeant of the Year and the Green Beret. Yep, one person, me, I'm the guy. So, how could I not leverage that to show I'm a high performer among high performers? It would be blatantly stupid on my part. I'd earned the right to those titles and awards. More importantly, highlighting this time in my career for the possible reward was worth the risk. Not to mention, what the hell would I put on my resume for that time? Skip it and say, "Hey, don't look here," or make something up?

Now to come full circle. When I got the job with my company, I spoke with my bosses about my resume and interviews. I'm on the inside; why not get some good feedback, right? The manager and final decision-maker said, "Man, the thing that stood out to me most, and why I knew we should hire you besides my leads saying 'hire this guy with no questions asked' was that you were a drill sergeant and how you showcased that on your resume and in your interview." Yep, pretty ironic. The moral of the story is that you own your journey. Maybe some people were turned off by that on my resume, and I'll never know, but I know I stayed true to the man in the mirror.

You will have your base document and will need to tailor it for each position you apply for. More on how to adapt and translate it in the next chapter. Again, there are many thoughts on the length of the resume. Let's break it down a little bit. Do you think anything you may have done 15, 22, or 31 years ago is relevant to a job you're applying for today? My best guess is it's not unless you know the person seeing the resume worked there also, maybe. I would leave it off or have a short amount of information for any work experience that is over ten years old unless it is directly relevant to the job. On the flip side, if you went straight into the military right out of high school or college and served for 4–8 years, do you think you have enough to fill up two pages or a page and a half? Okay, filled up with relevant information? I'm going to say probably not.

RESUME FORMAT SUGGESTION

- ► Heading
- ► Objective or Summary
- ► Experience
- ► Education
- ► Skills/ Certifications
- ► Activities/ Interests or Personal

HEADING

Your heading should consist of your NAME (in big, bold letters to stand out), address (minimum of town and state), phone number, email, and LinkedIn URL. No need for any more or less information.

OBJECTIVE/SUMMARY

A paragraph that highlights your relevant skills and capabilities at first glance. Think of it as similar to your elevator pitch typed out with slightly more detail. You could list some additional skills also.

EXPERIENCE

You list your positions chronologically from the current position down to the oldest. Minus the current position, everything should be written in the past tense. You can list your job, duty station, and dates. Keep it to no more than four relevant bullets per position. You will probably struggle to find more than that per position. Also, keep the bullets to no more than two lines each. It helps the reader if it is not all jumbled with words, and there is open white space to make it easier on their eyes. Going past around ten years ago, I recommend having just one relevant bullet. What you did then is less important than what you did two years ago. It will be covered in the next chapter, but every bullet should give all the information needed: what happened, how you did it, and what were the results. Making the data quantifiable is the best way for someone to try to understand what you mean (i.e., Selected 1st out of 500 other sailors is pretty easy to figure out.)

EDUCATION

Like on LinkedIn, list your educational degrees and graduate programs. If you had a very high GPA, you could include it, but it is not necessary. Don't add it if it is low. You're selling yourself here, no need to offer them your warts.

SKILLS/CERTIFICATIONS

Use this section to add any additional skills you may have, like language, graphic arts, or computer coding. Same with any relevant certifications that you earned and put on your LinkedIn.

ACTIVITIES/INTERESTS OR PERSONAL

Some people call this last portion by a different name and put varying information. To me, this is a secret weapon to use when a person is going to be reading your resume. This is a chance to make a human connection jump off the piece of paper. You can list community service that you do—that's usually a "good person" thing to do and a conversation piece. What I recommend is using this area for anything that didn't fit elsewhere, and you think it will help you. Hence my use of the phrase "secret weapon."

If you have seen a picture of me, you can guess that I'm not a small person. I'm around 6ft and 250lbs with longer hair and a big ole beard. As you now know, I was a drill sergeant and a Green Beret. Let's be real about what that can mean. People might have a misconception that I'm going to be one of the biggest assholes walking through the door on any given day. An assistant dean at one of our country's top business schools told me, "Herb, you are one intimidating man." Nothing you can do but laugh and say, "Come on! I'm a teddy bear." It is a bias to deal with. My personality is laid back, and I'm always smiling and laughing. I try to ensure that's visible in all social media posts in case anyone is looking. Okay, so now for the secret weapon. I always include that I like hiking in my free time with my Labradoodle Liberty Belle. Why? Well, for starters, it's true. My kids may have asked if I love the dog more than them... no comment. More importantly, I added this fact because it makes me look human and knocks down stereotypes and biases. It's an easy conversation starter, and who can't smile talking about a cool dog, including me. In every interview I did for graduate schools and jobs, which is over 15, I was asked about my Liberty Belle. Usually, it was the first thing that came up and started a great conversation with me being a human, not a soldier who went off to war and did bad things to bad people. Find your way to be human and jump off the page as a good person.

8

Translating Your Skills

DECISIONS THAT WE MADE years ago will stick with us and build a part of who we are. We can't hide from who we are. We have to highlight our strengths. Immediately out of high school, I joined the Army and served 20+ years. During this time, I earned my bachelor's degree in a non-traditional manner. I did not run from figuring out what I was going to do after the military. It helped shape who I am today. There may have been a brief moment of doubt as I began to consider top MBA programs in the country, which I felt I needed to meet my long-term goals. I sold myself as someone who was able to juggle life, the military, deployments, and maintain my studies with a few bumps in the road. I must have sold something correctly because I was accepted at one and waitlisted at two top-15 MBA programs in the country—not bad for a kid who barely passed high school because I didn't care and took online college classes. I was able to do this by selling my story in a cohesive manner that highlighted my strengths and made me stick out compared to others. What matters more than what you've done is how well you can craft that into an excellent narrative for a job or graduate school. I always say you need to be you, don't be someone else, or who you think they want you to be. Now let's get onto one of the toughest parts of the transition mission, translating your skills, capabilities, and experiences.

TIPS ON TRANSLATING YOUR SKILLS

▶ Use business terms, not military terms

▶ Quantify your data

▶ Avoid the stuff that you think is cool

▶ Identify proper language from job postings and informational interviews

▶ Trust your process and instincts

▶ Think how it is relevant to the job you're seeking

▶ You be you

THE ELEVATOR PITCH

This should be the first thing that comes out of translating your skills; towards the beginning of the transition. It will start out sounding like shit, but with time and all of your preparation, you will get this down. What is the elevator pitch? You step in an elevator and have the elevator ride to introduce yourself to someone—that is the intent behind it. The truth is, you have had practice at this—maybe not good practice—but practice none the less. When people asked you what you do for a living, you had a response. When you went back home to where you grew up, you were able to answer if people asked, "Hey, what have you been up too?" What makes it different now is one of these times it may lead to a person hiring you, making a key connection, or even just a person taking the time to help you on your journey.

This does not need to be overthought. Who are you, and where are you headed? I started out with something like, "Hi, I'm Herb Thompson, a retiring Special Forces team sergeant looking to take my experiences from solving problems in ambiguous situations to an opportunity in management consulting." Short and sweet and to the point. I was awesome. Then I realized I was not telling the information that I wanted or needed to. First, some people would get hung up on what is Special Forces. If I had a dollar for every time I heard, "Is that like the SEALs," I'd have a nice lake house. Second, I said I was a team sergeant, and in some cases, that led to the enlisted bias. Third, while it may sound neat to say, "My experiences solving problems in ambiguous situations," what the hell does that mean? At the end of the day, that leaves more questions than answers. I continued to refine my pitch to capture who I really am and where I wanted to be. It should not take you seven minutes to get that across to another person. They can always ask for further details and have a conversation. Your short elevator pitch is the hook to make it happen. Ask yourself, "What is relevant?" Develop and refine your elevator pitch. Then expand upon it. Be ready for situations where you have extra time. Just don't practice so much that you sound and look like a robot.

WAR STORIES ARE COOL, BUT...

Transitioning combat veterans possess excellent skills and experiences that can bring value to a new organization upon their transition out of the Army. Sharing these experiences is critical to networking and informing others about our skill sets. We all have cool war stories that we can tell. There was that time when we were surrounded and fought our way out. Remember when we survived that ambush and pushed our partner force to continue the mission? There was that time, back in that little no-name town in "X" country, where we got blown up by an IED and continued the mission. We infilled for an operation on a helicopter to a hot LZ and fought our way into a village to free it from insurgents. We dropped in from altitude for a gun run on insurgent positions. All great stories, but what do they portray?

People may want to hear these stories, and we may be willing to tell them in certain situations. But what will the person be understanding when we tell the story? Chances are they are going to be attracted to the shooting, blood, heroism, and sadness of the event. It's doubtful that they are hearing about the leadership you provided, cross-cultural communication, and problem-solving that the story also captured.

When telling these stories, we need to do preparation for the environment and think about what we want to be heard from our story. It is easy to get sucked into telling a cool war story. However, it probably does not convey our transferable skills in a clear and concise manner. The fact is, no one cares that we shot a weapon or closed with the enemy. This is what I like to call a sideshow, an entertaining 15 minutes that gets us nowhere or more than likely sets us back.

Highlight in your experiences the time that you worked by, with, and through the partner force to accomplish the mission—the numerous times you solved problems in an ambiguous situation without all the information and achieved mission success—the quantifiable results. Talk about the time you had to coach a junior member of the team or a foreign leader to improve their leadership and operations, or the time you innovated a solution to a problem that affected a whole village, your unit, or area. Remember the time you negotiated with village elders or militia members? These are examples of stories that show our transferable skill sets and will leave people thinking I could see this guy in my organization.

So next time you have an opportunity to share your experiences, think about the message that you are transmitting. How will it be received by the listener? A little tweak on what we highlight can make a significant difference in how we are perceived. Have an opening to grab their attention, an interesting middle, and an ending that reaches a climax and solidifies your point of the story. Don't be a sideshow, or as one retired Green Beret told me, a "neat-o" or their unicorn.

A THOUGHT EXPERIMENT

Photo Courtesy of the U.S. Army

What do you see in the above picture?
(Don't look at the next paragraph.)

_____

_____

_____

_____

_____

Now, I'll explain what you may not see in the above picture.

They worked closely with senior management to provide relevant analysis and strategic recommendations that resulted in the acceptance of a $1.2 million project bid. They led the 27-person team in developing a winning value proposition that exceeded the needs of the customer by 25% and saw four stakeholders increase investment by 40%.

SAMPLE BULLETS

► Selected over 500 other soldiers for a high level of competency and discipline.

► Managed a move of $15 million in equipment over 7,000 miles, saved 15% in transportation costs.

► Conducted 25 meetings with key stakeholders in a foreign country, gained their trust and approval for 11 community safety projects.

► Worked closely with Senior Management to provide relevant analysis and strategic recommendations that resulted in the acceptance of a $1.2 million project bid.

► Spearheaded effort to rewrite and update doctrine that outlined training procedures to the Army; incorporated all elements of general's staff and six separate military installations.

EXAMPLE JOB POSTINGS

(Note the highlighted words.)

As the **Senior Business Operations Analyst**, you will plan and direct **organizational, financial,** and **operational activities** for the Leader of Hosting Services. You will **arrange** and **prioritize critical issues** and **required information** to facilitate **efficient decision making**, as well as serve as a strategist, consultant, and implementer to achieve **streamlined activities** within the organization based on urgency and priority. In this role, you will **deliver insight** and **make recommendations** to help **Infrastructure Services** accomplish the **vision** and **strategic deliverables** for the organization.

The **Change Management and Training Consultant/Specialist** will be supporting an effort to create a **new organizational design** for a human resources office at a federal agency. This individual **will work with a team** to accomplish the following:

- ► Support **requirements gathering, scoping,** and **undertaking change impact analysis** work on current programs

- ► Identifying communication and training needs and developing appropriate materials using Next-Generation Communication tools (e.g., Adobe InDesign, etc.)

- ► Owning and supporting the development of deployment and adoption plans and ensuring the successful handover of the transformation into business as usual

- ► Liaise with key stakeholders as requested by the client's organization and conduct key stakeholder meetings to gather and provide information

- ► Assess current organizational state and use data to make recommendations

- ► Work with the team to develop a plan for implementation of new organizational structure

An organization that's growing extremely fast and looking to bring a **Supply Chain Manager** to their Operations team! The ideal candidate will be reporting/working directly with the **COO** as well as the **Operations department**. This person will have no direct reports but will be the **lead Supply Chain contact throughout the organization**.

Responsibilities Required:

- ► Provide **daily leadership, direction,** and **priorities** to procurement and **demand planning team**

- ► **Manage activities related** to **strategic** or **tactical purchasing, material requirements planning, inventory control, warehousing,** or **receiving**

- ► Place **purchase orders** in support of **customer orders** and **business forecast**

- ► Provide **regular communication** on critical **supplier deliveries, proactive communication** on changes

- ► Support **daily** and **weekly meetings** to ensure **clear communication** on parts and service delivery

- ► Provide **hands-on support in cycle counting, receiving inspection, warehouse** or other areas of the business as needed

- ► **Monitor supplier performance** to **assess the ability** to meet **quality** and **delivery requirements**

- ► **Analyze information** about supplier performance or procurement program success

- ► **Meet with suppliers** to discuss performance **metrics,** to **provide performance feedback,** or to discuss **production forecasts** or changes

- ▶ Collaborate with other departments, such as production, engineering, accounting, and quality assurance, to **identify** or **qualify new suppliers**

- ▶ **Negotiate prices and terms** with suppliers, vendors, or freight forwarders

- ▶ Establish cycle counting process; **perform routine cycle counts** to ensure inventory accuracy

- ▶ Establish **obsolete inventory process**; provide regular reporting and recommendations on obsolete inventory to ensure optimal use of system for current state and future state of business

- ▶ Support operational **KPIs: safety, quality, delivery, efficiency, inventory**

- ▶ Document **supply chain processes**, such as **workflows, cycle times, position responsibilities,** or **system flows**

- ▶ **Provide new and innovative solutions** to im**prove workflow** and **customer fulfillment**

- ▶ **Analyze inventories** to determine how to **increase inventory turns, reduce waste,** or **optimize customer service**

- ▶ Flexible hours to support daily customer commitments

Above are sample job postings for real jobs. Highlighted are the keywords that should stick out to you as you read them. If you were applying for one of these jobs or in one of these industries, you would need to have a number of these words in your resume, and more importantly, be able to talk about them in your interview. Your interview prep, along with the resume refinement, should incorporate as many of these words as possible, and they should flow in conversations easily. You will not hit all of them, but the more of them that you can seamlessly include, the more qualified for the position you will look. I'm not saying to lie, but it is tough for one to check whether you did all of this, so if you did something very similar, and it can be characterized in these terms, then change your words to sound more relevant. You must be prepared to talk about them and know what you're talking about. Lying will lead to you showing your faults later on, and you may get terminated.

ENLISTED BIAS

(A perspective I previously wrote regarding Green Berets, but there is a lot of carryover for others. Included are five characteristics that I was promoting for my brothers.)

For enlisted Special Forces soldiers transitioning out of the Army: a word of caution. Despite an increased understanding of our training, role, and mission, there is still a nagging stereotype for enlisted versus officers. While internally, we have our knowledge of NCOs and team sergeants and their importance on a team, there's much more educating to do in the private sector.

My first experience with this issue was at my first and last job fair that I attended a year ago. I walked in looking sharp, resumes in hand, and elevator pitch ready to go. I spoke with a few people milling around, talked to a few companies, and decided to approach a company that I had minimal interest in but thought it was a chance to practice my elevator pitch.

I introduced myself as a soon-to-be retiring Special Forces Team Sergeant and continued. The gentleman from this company said, "Nice to meet you. You would be great in our warehouse." He elaborated slightly, and I could tell he was not talking about a supply chain manager or warehouse manager job. A lot of emotions and thoughts went through my mind the instant he said that: anger, surprise, frustration, and humor—to name a few. I thanked him for his time, and as I walked away, I overheard a junior officer introduce himself to the company. They started talking about rotational leadership positions and management opportunities.

Now, all work is noble, and I'm sure there was no offense intended in his statement. However, as a Green Beret, just months ago, I was leading a team that was an integral part of a multi-billion-dollar operation while working across cultures and languages. We had multiple stakeholders across an array of countries with my actions impacting decisions up to the strategic level and the National Security Council. You're right! I would be great in your warehouse. It would become the best operating warehouse in the history of warehouses on a cheap wage.

Like other enlisted Special Forces soldiers, I have had to solve countless problems in ambiguous situations with lives on the line or with U.S. national policy implications at stake. The ability to work cross-functionally across cultures had been tested and proven on countless missions. Having led teams ranging in size from 2 to over 200, I've been able to hone my leadership skills by making a connection with people. I had proven my flexibility and ability to adapt under high-stress situations.

What was evident to me at that point was one thing: there is a misunderstanding about the military and especially Special Forces Non-Commissioned Officers. I could whine about it and become disgruntled with this lack of understanding, but like every Green Beret, I believe in generating solutions to problems, not hiding from them. Educating people is the way to close that information gap.

The fact is when Green Berets deploy, these NCOs often have responsibilities on par or exceeding their conventional officer counterparts. Each of these can and often lead and/or advise a company-size force of over 100 foreign fighters. With no formal chain of command structure to follow like conventional forces, these men have to earn the respect of their counterparts and use all of their interpersonal skills to accomplish the mission. This all takes place in a foreign language, in a different culture, and often under challenging circumstances. Special Forces NCOs thrive in this environment and can do the same in any organization or business.

Enlisted SF NCOs need to translate our experiences in a way that shows our value. Our SF officers need to spread the word about our importance. Our trusted advocates out there across America need to talk to others about our merit. If all of these people translate and educate others about our value, we will be successful.

For the prospective employers out there, there are some nuances in how Special Forces enlisted team members can stand out on your private sector team. They bring five characteristics of who they are and what they have honed over time in countries around the world.

Special Forces veterans are known for their problem-solving ability around the world. These NCOs have had to solve problems in ambiguous situations where the results were life or death. Their training and experience with their planning process allow them to approach problems uniquely. These are the guys that you want on your team to develop solutions, no matter the problem. If you hire these individuals, they will develop solutions for you.

These NCOs are highly adaptable. They have proven their ability to work cross-functionally and across cultures on missions spanning the globe. When these men are put into situations, they are the tip of the spear for U.S. Armed Forces and policy. They have had to be flexible and fill multiple roles to succeed. One minute they may be negotiating with a tribal elder, the next they are training a foreign force to protect their community, and then they may be briefing a U.S. ambassador alongside foreign dignitaries on the ground truth of a given country. You can count on these Green Berets to take on a multitude of tasks.

Because these Special Forces NCOs have worked by, with, and through a foreign partner force, they have developed a high level of emotional intelligence. Their ability to build rapport and read people in a short period has kept them alive and enabled them to achieve mission success. Few people in the workforce have mastered this skill as much as an SF NCO. They are masters of the human domain. Their ability to empathize and relate with a wide variety of people is what has allowed them to succeed around the world with indigenous forces. These men will be able to read the people around your organization and adjust decisions based on the ground truth.

Men going through SF selection, qualification, and missions have proven their grit. These men will not quit. They will ensure the mission is accomplished. The NCOs of Special Forces will not be deterred by a bad day or a tough deal. They will keep going until they have a solution for your organization. You can count on them to continue working in your business until you meet your goals.

Lastly, these men are force multipliers. Quite simply, they make others better. They have spent a career going overseas in small teams and empowering much larger forces to improve their capabilities. They will get in your company and improve your team. These Green Berets will enhance your company from within.

Note: I included this article, which I had previously written, for a few reasons. (Yes, there is carryover to other military careers.) I wanted to show how these people bring value, and I gave examples that people can understand. I identified a problem and offered some solutions. Writing this article was a positive way to vent and make a difference. It just took a little bit of time and thought, and now it's out on the inter-webs for anyone to see.

I want to leave you with this one last thought about translating your skills. You have a number of soft skills, the intangibles. You are a leader. Good luck finding a job description that says hiring a leader. The private sector is not the same as military service. People are not in leadership positions, per se. I'll add that just about every other veteran will sell themselves as leaders. What is going to set you apart from the competition is not focusing on leadership and some of those other soft skills. You still need the hard skills required for the job. That is what you need to sell them. I look at it like a cake. The soft skills are the icing—you can't just have icing. That alone doesn't make a cake. You need the cake made up of the hard skills. Then the icing matters on top of those hard skills. Translate your experience into the hard skills that they require then add a little icing. Don't just hand them a container of icing and a spoon.

This chapter was just meant to get you pointed in the right direction, just like the rest of the book. It is up to you to do the legwork and figure out the best solutions for you, your situation, and your goals. Stretch yourself as far as possible and become comfortable with the uncomfortable. What your unit or section did provides no value to the company; they need to see and hear what you can do for them.

9

Your Targeted Companies

TIPS FOR YOUR TARGETS

► Network into the company via a connection or trusted person

► Research the Hiring Manager via Google searches and LinkedIn

► Utilize Glassdoor and similar sites to find specifics on the company and possibly the team's culture

► If given the opportunity to interview in person, speak with as many people from the company as possible. Engage the receptionists, janitors, the random person walking down the hall, anybody and everybody

► Get a real feel for the organization

► Attempt to speak with people who have left the company, identify any recurring themes

You have done all the preparation and determined you want to work at a specific company in your new industry. Your networking has got you in the door. This is what you have been waiting for—the moment to show your value. Through hard work and struggle, you now have a resume that is top-notch. People in the company are pulling for you and have put in a good word on your behalf. Your dream job is at your fingertips. Nothing can stop you now!

REJECTION

Time to get punched in the face. Your dream job does not love you like you love it. You feel you did well in the interview, while not perfect, you articulated your value and walked out with a bounce in your step. Then, nothing happened. No call back the next day with a job offer or an opportunity for the second interview. It's okay. They are just dotting their I's and crossing their T's. A week later—nothing—and you followed up with a nice and concise email thanking them for the interview opportunity and how excited you were to learn more about their company. Ding, you have an email. The email states, "Thank you for interview. While you are an impressive candidate for this position and our company, we have decided to move forward in the process with other candidates." No, it can't be right. This is your dream, and they know how much you want it. The very harsh reality that we all experience is REJECTION. Except for the very few who are lucky, you will be rejected. You will not hear back from a company, maybe not even get an interview for your dream job (not likely if you followed the plan).

Maybe have a drink and sulk for a night. Get the emotions of the failure out of you. Out of this failure rises success. Use it for the lessons learned on the journey and turn it into fuel for your fire. Reanalyze the interview and all communications with the company. There are times when it is just not meant to be. Other times, you may see where you did not show your value in the best way and can learn from it. The most important thing to realize is this is not the end of the world; all of your brothers and sisters go through the same thing.

No one likes rejection. You have hated it since you asked out your first crush to the sock hop dance in the 5th grade, only to be crushed when they said they were going with someone else. I talk about this because it is real and very likely to happen to you. There is a high probability that you will not get the job at the first place you attempt. Now for the good news: you will succeed. One of the best traits you take out of the military is grit. Time to get to work.

MY FIRST REJECTION

After doing all of my planning, soul searching, and come to Jesus moments—I had found my path. I knew my dream. I was going to start my own management consulting business for small and medium-sized companies to compete against the giants like Amazon and Walmart. To get there, I realized I had a little bit of a knowledge/skills gap—and being a former Green Beret and drill sergeant would not instantly create confidence in the businesses I was trying to help and market myself to. So, I knew I needed to make a stop at a top tier MBA program. Only the best would work. I came to learn about the Tuck School of Business at Dartmouth. This was my dream. Truth is, it became my driving challenge and consumed all of my free time. I would not fail! The guy who was the first in his family to get a bachelor's degree (and got online) was going to make it in the Ivy League.

Just like it was a mission, and what I have put forth in this book, I pursued it with everything I had. Over a year, I made three trips to Hanover, NH from my home in Tennessee. I networked my ass off, talking with over 200 Tuckies. I did the Tuck: Next Step Transition to Business program (I believe this to be the best transition program available). I paid to have a tutor and took the GRE three times. I was getting in! Because of my grit and tenacity, at least three current students and alumni had submitted extra letters of recommendation.

I had done it all. All I needed to do now was to wait for the day that they made the first-round acceptance calls. I waited all day. Nothing happened, no call. This couldn't be right. I knew they loved me as much as I loved them. Then I got the email. It started with, "We congratulate you for being placed on the waitlist…" I was shocked and heartbroken. I did not have a backup plan. I did not listen as others told me to apply elsewhere or consider top-tier EMBA programs. I had put all of my eggs in this basket, and I failed. All my training and experience told me to have contingency plans, and I did not have one. After a night of sulking and maybe a few stiff drinks to boot, I reassessed my plan. I talked with mentors and friends. They reminded me of my accomplishments—a poor kid with an online degree who was retiring as an E-8 from the U.S. Army had been accepted to the waitlist at a top-ten Ivy League MBA program. Everything I had learned during this process, I would use to adjust my plan. Small victories.

MY SECOND REJECTION

My dream had not changed, just how I would get there did. I would do my EMBA at a top-tier program and go to work for a great company. One of my three targeted companies was a tech startup focused on defense issues. My Special Forces teammates were two of the company's first 40 employees. They were located on the west coast, and I did not want to move west, but they had a small office in Washington, DC. My brothers set me up for an interview with the guy in charge of the DC office. I flew up to DC and was ready to rock his world. I went to their office and met this gentleman. We talked for a little over an hour. As I left, he said I'll talk with some other people in the company, and then we'll get back in touch. I knew I had done very well, not perfect, but I was me and showed my value to the company as we talked over their upcoming venture. I was pretty pumped up. This could be an exciting job with a really good company, doing things that mattered, and I'd even get to work with a few of my brothers. I called my buddy the next day, and he told me it didn't go very well. The guy who did the interview gave me about an 85% grade, and I was just not right for what they were looking for at this time. I was floored. I could not believe it. At a place where two people very close to me were championing me, I could not get the job. There was no hope for me at a place where people didn't know me. I was never going to find anything but a meaningless, mundane job. I was never going to make anything above some hourly wage. It was a rough weekend. I did not want to become a statistic.

OUT OF FAILURE RISES SUCCESS

The truth is these rejections were some of the best things to happen to me on my journey. They were learning moments for me to reassess where I was going and how I could get there. It made me work harder on articulating my value proposition to a new company. I improved how I translated my skills. I networked more to better understand how to convey what I knew in my head: I'm a top-notch applicant that anyone should want to hire. I'm full of real-world experiences under the harshest and most ambiguous situations. I just had to refine my approach and my sales pitch.

From these failures came my acceptance to the EMBA program at Cornell University, where the dean of the SC Johnson Graduate School of Management called me on a Saturday after I was accepted to ensure that I was actually going to come to the school. These failures led to my successful interviews with companies like Deloitte and Accenture, which led to me accepting a position at Accenture

Federal. I talk about these failures and my successes not to say, "Oh, look at me," but to show you that you will be rejected, but with grit and a positive attitude, you will find your success.

THE INTERVIEWS

One of the most overlooked aspects of transition and the job hunt is the interview. You need to practice this! This is actually the most important component of the hiring process. Ensure you have 4–6 situations broken down into the STAR approach. Situation about 20%, Task about 15%, Actions 40%, and Results 25%. There are other ways, but this is a foolproof method to succinctly relay all necessary information. Practice it on a number of responses. It will be impossible for you to know every question you will be asked, but you can be prepared to answer any question knowing the STAR method, and you will know how you can translate your experience. Practice with a friend who is also transitioning. Check out the non-profit Candorful, which does mock interviews. Consider the people you built relationships with through networking. Who may be willing to give you a mock interview? Do yourself a favor, and do not ignore this crucial step.

Most people put so much time, effort, and maybe even money into their resumes and then ignore the interviews. I'm going to give you another secret: the interviews are what get you the job! Yes, you need the resume, as we have discussed. Yes, you have to network your ass off to get the interview at your targeted company. Now it is just you and someone else on the phone, a virtual chat, or in the room, conducting the first of what most likely will be several interviews. This is what will land you the job that you dream of. Everything has built to this moment.

Please do not ignore your interview preparation. It is probably the most important part of the process. You need to be able to succinctly articulate why YOU will bring them value and how YOU can alleviate any risks they may see in hiring you. This isn't about your old team. This isn't about your old rank. This isn't about anything other than you. There are some ways to be prepared to knock their socks off.

INTERVIEW TIPS

► Relax

► Be yourself, not who you think they want you to be

► Have 4–6 stories from your past ready to answer questions they have for you

► You can never know every question they will ask you

► Use the STAR method

► Dress the part

► Make all of your answers relevant to the job and company

► Do your best to research your interviewer

► Don't be a robot, have a personality

► Follow up

You have made it to the interview stage. You are almost to the finish line. You belong in this interview, and you belong with this company. Take a deep breath. No one knows your value and what you can bring to this company better than you. Smile and keep on smiling. Be seen as human and someone they would want to work next to for eight hours a day. Can they picture being stuck on an airplane or in the airport for a five-hour layover with you? Your goal is to make them think they would enjoy that experience. More than likely, they will start by asking you to talk about yourself. This is a layup! Yes, they want to get to know you a little more, but also, it's a chance for you to talk about what you know best and settle in. Have your short pitch ready to go that summarizes where you came from and where you are going. No need to talk about that time in high school that you did something silly. Keep it on point and relevant. This should be a conversation; don't just talk and keep talking. Get across the necessary details, and they can ask for more information or clarity.

My goal was to have a theme for each interview. Why? Well, if I geared the interviews towards one or two themes, it would be easier for the interviewer to walk away with a theme that I had laid out for them. For example, in my current role, I had a couple of themes in my separate interviews. In one interview, I focused on my ability to build relationships and connect with customers. This theme stuck out with my boss, and that is what she was drawn to. In another, I talked about my passion to bring efficiencies and processes to my clients. This stuck out with one of my bosses. In another, I talked about my ability to train people. If the goal is to get them to see you in the role you're interviewing for, then they should walk away thinking, "Yes, this is the right person for the job." If you are all over place, talking about 15 different tasks that you're great at—a combat story, that one time in training, and then the 27 awesome ways you can bring value to the company—they will be confused. Sounds silly but keep it simple. You don't know what questions they will ask, but you can have your four to six stories ready to go that can be shaped in different ways. Think of some experiences or stories that could answer the following questions with a few tweaks in how you tell it.

INTERVIEW QUESTIONS

- ► Tell me about yourself.

- ► What are your strengths?

- ► What are your weaknesses?

- ► Tell me about a time that you had to build a team.

- ► Tell me about a time that you influenced others.

- ► Tell me about a time that you overcame difficulties.

- ► I'm sure you have made mistakes. Tell me about one that you've grown from.

- ► How do you connect with a customer?

- ► What skills are you bringing to our team?

These questions are not the end all be all of interview questions. They should be enough to get your creative juices flowing and have your go-to answers ready. Remember to use the STAR format for just about any question. Is it easier to comprehend when you tell them a skill/experience you have or when you give them a short 2-minute story using the STAR method? The succinct story in the STAR method wins every day of the week. It's also okay if you're missing something in your experiences for this job. You may get asked about that. Show them that you understand you're lacking in that area but are a quick learner or can overcome in other ways. However, if you have to say that numerous times, this may not be the job for you. Bottom line, if you're not confident in your abilities for this job, how are they going to want to hire you?

Another item to think about is your questions for them. Yes, that's right, you're also interviewing them. Have two to three questions ready to go that are not easy to find with a quick internet search or by spending two minutes on the company website. Some examples may be: What is the day to day operation like? How have you been able to move up in the company? I personally like to ask: Is there anything about me that gives you concern about this position? Or, how do you see me fitting in here? It puts them on the spot. They can lie, which would be a sign. More than likely, they will respond with a good barometer of where you stand, and then there will be no need to walk out wondering how you have done.

YOU GOT A JOB OFFER

This is awesome news. It's what you have been waiting to hear. My suggestion: don't accept it immediately. It's like the first person you asked out who said yes; did you end up marrying them? Maybe you did, and it worked out like a fairytale, but chances are, your life took a different path. Take a little time to be sure this is the right one vs. just the first one. I turned down a job offer or two. They were not what I wanted, but I would have accepted them if I needed to put food on my table. Take your time to understand what the job is, and if it is the right situation for you and your family. If you do decide to take the job, it's not just a simple yes. There can and should be a negotiation for your compensation and benefits.

HOW NOT TO NEGOTIATE

I received the job offer to the place I wanted to work. This was it for me. I got the offer detailing my compensation and benefits in an email and then talked it over on the phone with a company representative. The pay was more than I could have ever dreamed of. The job had a good amount of days off, great benefits for all employees, and I could start on the date of my choosing. Now the cons were no bonus, no money for my schooling, and all the benefits were standard—no dog at work for me. I pondered this for a few minutes, thinking back to my goals and how happy I was for this offer. I wanted to be a team player and come in with others knowing I didn't pinch every penny I could for my services. I accepted what they offered me without a negotiation and was extremely pleased. The truth is, I probably failed myself and my family in some ways. I more than likely could have gotten more money and a bonus if I had just pushed back the slightest bit.

Once I started working and had been with the company for a little while, I realized something I had not ever thought of. Just about no one knows each other's salary. So, my trying to be a good team player was a waste. No one talks about how much they make. In the military, it was never a question because we have a standard wage scale based upon our grade and time in service. Same rank and same time in service means the same pay. In the private sector, the salaries for employees can vary even when people are doing the same job. The only thing I did by not asking for more money or a bonus was give myself a zero chance of getting more compensation. I didn't even push it to ask, so there was no way for them to say no or agree and pay me more. Don't do what I did. They offered you the position. They are not taking that offer back because you ask for 10% more in salary or in a bonus, which may be easier for them to justify. You don't know what will happen unless you ask.

OTHER AREAS TO CONSIDER FOR NEGOTIATION

- ► Pay
- ► Bonus
- ► Paid time off
- ► Continuing education benefits

► Flexible work hours

► Remote work/work from home

► Stock options (if a public company)

► Work start date

► Bring your dog to work

Are you concerned about what your salary is and how it would compare to other locations? I recently talked with a transitioning Army Special Forces Captain. After receiving an offer, he reached out to me to talk about whether or not he should negotiate for more or if he was getting what he should. Since we had talked multiple times, I knew a lot of what his "why" and goals were. So, I said, "Let's just look at the pay." There are multiple tools out there that will make comparisons based on the cost of living expenses. I showed him a tool on Nerd Wallet's cost of living calculator to compare salaries in two cities. As an example, $100,000 in Charlotte, NC on Nerd Wallet was $158,000 in Arlington, VA. The large difference might amaze you. Nerd Wallet goes into how they calculate their cost of living. On my journey, I used a different method. I stuck to what I knew: DoD Basic Allowance for Housing rates. I figured, with how much money was involved, the DoD must have a pretty good methodology down to determine their rates. In 2019, an O-3 with dependents in Charlotte gets $1,851 monthly, compared to $2,745 in Arlington, VA. With some quick math, that means the pay in Arlington, VA is 148% greater than Charlotte, NC. A salary of $100,000 would equal a salary of $148,000 in Arlington, VA. That is a little less than the Nerd Wallet's calculation. It would sound a lot better to be getting paid $148,000 than $100,000. But with that extra salary comes a higher cost of living. Doing this process may give you a new perspective on a salary that is offered.

10

It's a Technique

————

WHILE I WAS DEPLOYING on my transition mission, I decided to try a few tests to see what would happen if I had not planned as much as I had, or if I chose a different approach. Daily, over a couple of months, I applied to positions, sometimes up to 100 in a day. If I was more of an analytical person, I would have captured better data on my applications. But I know I applied to over 1,000 jobs. The number is probably closer to 1,500 jobs. Admittedly, these were not my targeted jobs, but you never know what might happen. I used LinkedIn, Indeed, ZipRecruiter, and company websites.

All of these jobs were in a salary range of $60,000 to $120,000. There were a number of job titles and industries, to name a few: Program Manager, Management Consultant, Business Development, Customer Service Representative, Financial Advisor, Operations Manager, Training and Leadership Development, and Business Analyst. The majority were in the zone of consideration for me. I may have been over and under-qualified for a small number of the positions. Most just required my resume. I'm guessing less than 25% required me to answer four to ten questions. If the job posting required more than that amount of work, I didn't apply for it. This was for a test. I wasn't crazy enough to waste that much of my time. I used a resume that was very similar to the ones I used for my targeted companies and did not tailor it to each of these jobs.

Now the results from that work, or more appropriately, lack thereof. I received back around 200 emails stating something along the lines of "while qualified, we are choosing to move forward with other candidates." These emails also included statements like "we have received your application but are not moving forward with the hiring process." Roughly less than 20% of companies even bothered to respond with a "not today soldier." I received less than 20 emails requesting an interview. This means that less than 1% of the jobs that I applied to for the test thought me worthy of an interview. This number includes a couple of companies that emailed me up to six-months later. I chose to do some of these interviews for practice. Why not get something besides validating a hypothesis? These interviews were great mock interviews because they were real live interviews. I ended up doing two or three with a couple of the companies and got a handful of job offers. What do you think happened then? You betcha, I negotiated for more compensation and benefits. Again, another chance to practice. Yes, if you have a decent memory, you are correct—even though I "practiced" a couple of real negotiations—I still messed up my actual negotiation. Never said I was perfect.

I know another veteran, Eric Horton, who is an amazing resource in helping those transitioning out. He did a similar test with much better data. He submitted over 1,200 applications to Project Manager, Program Manager, Operations Manager, and Business Development positions. Eric received responses from 5% of the companies. The percent of companies that offered him interviews was, ready for it, drum roll please, less than 1%. This is from a guy who was successful in transition, using a lot of the techniques I discuss in this book, and now his career is helping soldiers during their transition.

Eric knows what a resume is supposed to look like. I have come to learn what a resume is supposed to look like. Both of us had less than a 1% success rate in landing interviews by just submitting applications blindly to companies. That is astonishing, but also disheartening. Had I not put the effort into my transition, I would have thought this was the way to get a job. An overwhelming number of service members who are getting out of the military think this is the way to succeed. When they don't succeed, you can now understand why they are so many disgruntled and angry veterans. I'm not condoning their negative attitude, but this helps shine a light on maybe why they feel the way they do. Don't be one of them. Choose not to spray and pray.

Final Thoughts

⎯⎯⎯⎯⎯

A S I HAVE COVERED, in a lot of ways, the transition mission is the hardest deployment you ever hopped on. This book covers a large majority of that process to give you a jumping-off point for success. Successfully transforming into a civilian depends upon how much you work at it and your attitude. You can do this; countless brothers and sisters are at the ready to help. The key thing is they don't know you need help unless you pop a star cluster or smoke grenade. Reach out to others. Transition is a team sport. Do not go it alone in isolation. There are no Rambos. That only works in the movies.

I did not go into clearing the military or using the VA amongst a variety of other issues. There are many other sources available on those topics. If you follow the process laid out for you with your own tweaks, you will find those answers too. The one thing I will say is you have earned it! Use the VA to get what you've earned. It is not fun and can be a pain in the ass but get your ratings. Get the help. Don't become a statistic. Find what drives you to remain vertical and use that to fuel you through the tough times in seeking out help. For me, that was my two sons. I want to be here to see them grow up to be men of character. You earned the right to receive your care and disability compensation from the VA. Uncle Sam got everything it could out of you; return the favor and leverage the benefits paid for with your blood, sweat, and tears.

Utilize whatever your service offers for transition, but don't rely solely upon it. Our military is designed to win our Nation's wars, and because of patriots like you, we are very good at that. The military knows jack squat about not being in the military; reach outside the walls of your service for transition help. Everyone has to go through their services transition program. Use this as a starting point, but it is not the endpoint. You probably already figured this out considering you purchased this book. Our military is great at military tasks and exists to win our nation's wars. The military does not exist to make your transition successful. In the big picture, DoD is concerned about the money they have to earmark towards unemployment benefits for those who do not successfully transition. Do not rely solely upon your local military transition program. Move outside the walls of your base. In our digital age, this is easier than ever. Leverage every asset you can.

There are many great internship programs available as you come off of active duty. I did not write about these, because they did not fit into my plan. I've spoken with many who have leveraged these internships into a full-time job. Some learned that what they thought they wanted to do was not for them. Explore these opportunities in depth during your research and informational interviews. They're excellent opportunities to leverage.

Talk with your leadership about your transition and your plan for success. Some are more supportive than others. We could discuss this issue for hours. Control what you can control. You're working on selling yourself and pitching a new you. A good place to start is with your leadership. If needed or possible, explain what you are doing and the importance of your efforts. You can continue to do your mission and plan for the transition mission. The closer you get to clearing, the less you should be working, and the more you should be transitioning. Like I have previously stated, do not get sucked into work because they "need you." They will survive, and you need to focus on your post-military survival. Don't hurt your family and yourself by thinking the unit cannot survive without you.

I recommend that you take a knee or tactical pause when you exit the military. Now you may not be in a position to do this, but if you can, take advantage of the opportunity. You only get one brain and one family, neither is easily replaced. One of the best things I did in my transition was to take a few months off. The adjustment was awkward at first, but then I became rejuvenated. I was able to reconnect with my kids and spend even more time reflecting on my life. It may sound good to double dip and earn some extra money, but you can always make more money. Think of the long-term benefits of taking some time for yourself.

You'll notice this book didn't cost much more than a fancy cup of coffee at Starbucks or a drink at the local bar. This was done for one reason: so that there was no barrier to getting this book in your hands. I've helped hundreds in their transition, but I want to help more. What I ask of you is to pay it forward. Give back and help others. We all have busy lives, but the only thing stopping you from helping someone else is your decision not to. Think of where you would be if everyone decided not to help a fellow veteran. The time, money, and effort put into this book will be worth it if I know it helped one person.

Just like the intent of this book, I ask that you pay it forward. If this book helped you, think about getting one for someone coming behind you. If you didn't like this book (which I doubt it if you're still reading at one of the last pages), then do something else for those following in your footsteps. We are a brother and sisterhood. Take a moment to help others along the way and especially once you have found that comfort level in your deployment.

Reach out on LinkedIn at **linkedin.com/in/herb-thompson-sf2biz** or via email at **director@sf2biz.com**. I look forward to hearing about your successes or pondering your questions. I'll do my best to respond as soon as possible. If you're an organization wanting to purchase in bulk, contact me for a discount.

Own your journey!

Acknowledgments

I have to acknowledge those that helped me on this journey.

To Najdan, you did an impressive job bringing my vision to life for the cover.

To Jordana, your ability to edit and make me sound articulate while keeping it in my voice was impressive.

To the service members who seek me out, and who I speak with every week while you're on your transition mission—your determination and thirst for knowledge keep a fire lit in my belly to see you succeed and to keep giving back.

To the countless people who helped me on my transition mission without wanting anything in return, I would not be where I'm at today without your efforts and patriotism.

To my trusted agents, the ones who help me stay on azimuth, thank you for proofreading this book and the other articles I write. Your continuous ability to offer your time in putting up with my crazy ideas and providing me the candor that I value is priceless. It means I'll be there, no matter the time or situation, in support of you, my friends.

To Gavin, thank you for paying it forward with the crash course in marketing. You're an outstanding patriot and veteran.

To the leaders who took the time see my potential and mentor me along the way, thank you! Jack, Rob, Jerry, Nancy, Dean, and Dave—you have had more of an impact on my life then I can ever find the words to articulate.

To my sons that I'm not worthy of, you make me prouder and impress me more every day. Keep growing into the young men of character that you are becoming. I'll try my best not to mess that up. I appreciate your understanding that this book was about helping others and the values that this endeavor encapsulates.

We all help each other get better and grow.

Own your journey.

About the Author

HERB THOMPSON IS CURRENTLY a Management Consultant and Executive MBA student at Cornell University. He retired in March 2019 after over 20 plus years in the Army. He culminated his service as a Special Forces (Green Beret) Team Sergeant for 3.5 years in 5th Special Forces Group, The Legion. Prior to earning his Green Beret, he earned the 2008 U.S. Army Drill Sergeant of the Year award. He is the only person in the history of the Army to have earned this award and the Green Beret. Herb started his Army career in Human Resources as that was the only job available to him when he entered the Army as a color-blind 17-year-old. He earned a B.S. in Business Studies in Business Administration from Southern New Hampshire University online and attended the Tuck: Next Step Transition to Business graduate certificate program at the Tuck School of Business at Dartmouth. During his retirement from the Army, Herb founded SF2BIZ, a 501©3 organization with a mission to empower Special Forces veterans to seize opportunities in business. He currently resides at his slice of heaven in the woods in the Washington, DC area. In his free time, he supports veterans in transition, hikes with his spoiled Labradoodle Liberty Belle, and spends time with his two amazing young sons.